little she

First published in 2016 by Reed Independent, Victoria, Australia.

Printed by Createspace.com, a division of Amazon.com.

Available as a printed book or an ebook from Createspace.com or Amazon.com or Kindle estores, together with most major international online outlets or bookshops with online ordering facilities:
paperback: ISBN 9780994630124
ebook: ISBN 9780994630131

Front cover: Image from Google Images. Design by Dilani Priyangika Ranaweera, Dart Lanka Productions

National Library of Australia Cataloguing-in-Publication entry:
Creator: Reed, Bill, author.
Title: Little She/Bill Reed
Edition: first
ISBN: 9780994630124 (paperback)
ISBN: 9780994630131 (ebook)
Notes: includes bibliographical reference.
Subjects: Drama/female infanticide/black comedy
Dewey Number: A822.3

little she

a play

Bill Reed

R

Also by Bill Reed
Plays
Burke's Company
Bullsh/ More Bullsh
Cass Butcher Bunting
Mr Siggie Morrison with his Comb and Paper
Truganinni
Living in Black Holes (anthology)
Living on Mars (anthology)
Living on Mars: the play
Daddy the 8th
Truganinni Inside Out
Auntie and the Girl
Mirror, Mirror
Little She
You Want It, Don't You, Billy?
The Pecking Order
Jack Charles is Up and Fighting
Just Out of Your Ground
I Don't Know What to Do with You!
Paddlesteamer

novels
The Pipwink Papers\
Me, the Old Man
Stigmata
Ihe
Dogod
Crooks
Tusk
Throw her back
Are You Human?
Tasker Tusker Tasker
Awash
1001 Lankan Nights book 1
1001 Lankan Nights book 2
Passing Strange

Nonfiction
Water Workout

Award-winning short stories (see also title 'Passing Strange')
Messman on the C.E. Altar
The 200-year Old Feet
The Case Inside
Blind Freddie Among the Pickle Jars
The Old Ex-serviceman
The Shades of You my Dandenong

To the tiny ones who can't cry shame

Production Note

The play was written envisaging an adaption of a Son et Lumière presentation, with the narration being through READER SMITH, reading back his notes ostensibly to his wife.

The stage is set on two levels... at 'ground level' for the narration, then at the raised level where the 'play-out' takes place.

To heighten the son-et-lumière effect, READER SMITH can hold hand spotlights in addition to the scripts he is reading from. He can splay his own light on the presentation.

Overall, there is a giantish shape representing intermittently a presence of evil, overwhelming malevolence, the maddest of Kali incarnations, arguably Chinnamasta– and, indeed, the manic bull-horned manifestation of the priest NANDI BABA.

Overall, too, are the sounds of India... the traffic, the hubbub of people, the far-off temple bells, the dead of night, the whistling of eagles overhead.

The Characters

READER SMITH:
an Australian architect. Mid-40s. Quick to contrition; quick to
hotheadedness; prone to being always guilt-stricken. Most real
conversations he has ever had with his former partner would have
been confessionals... so that when, in a form of cowardice, he
writes to her about what happened in India rather than telling her
face-to-face, it just means his need to say sorry is endless.

SMITH:
the actor who plays READER SMITH on stage.

LAKSHMI SINGH:
Bollywood in heart and soul but larger-in-life. Mountainously,
both, she is in eternal dance and the world resonates with her.
That she speaks 'joke movie talk' gives her a great source of self-
amusement. She is wide-eyed, wide-girthed, wide-lipped. She is
absolutely sumptuous, and gorgeously knows it.

DR SINGH:
her husband. The town's Gynaecologist who runs the best
abortion clinic thereabouts and, of course and why-not?, is
municipal Coroner. Facetious one moment and fastidious the
next... but there is no way he would apply either when in front of
his adored wife.

NANDI BABA:
part-German Hindu priest/sadhu of the extreme wandering
Kapalika sect, whose adherents rave about the place – any place at
all! -- in order to show how life is a paradox that could never be a
paradox if you weren't so dopily paradoxical yourself. Either
European or Indian albino... and, anyway, either way, epicene. His
madcap German inflection is deliberately comical, a self-parody.
Mix'n'bake the nutty for a fruitcake.

ANNAPURNA:
the main smears on her filthy frock, around the pudenda regions,
are the stigmata of her six-year-old sick child she carries across

3

her chest. It is with fierce pride that she wears them these imprint stains. Unmarried, therefore socially spurned, in her eyes constitute a fierce resurrection, no matter what. As with her child outwardly, inwardly she carries a secret. Perfected English nails her as having a Christian convent upbringing.

LINGAYYA:
the area's Acting Superintendent of Police. Malevolence itself, as long as his handle-bar moustache, and not nearly so much as a joke. He'll lay into you before lacing you with questions. His smile and scowl comes as the wind goes, but survival is his rock bottom. His ancestry and elevated social place is his high – to everybody else's low.

The Setting

The son-et-lumiere lighting dominates the staging.

There is only one prop. This is a piece of furniture that is generally in shadow and which transfigures into a sitting platform, a bed, a crude 'altar' table etc.

Scenes are set by position on the stage area, rather than prop settings. As such, lighting is place-specific with actors often half-shadowy, or emerging from the shadows or being suddenly blacked-out.

Narration note

READER SMITH is the narrator. He reads from the 'manuscript' pages and diary and does so openly as part of the action. In this reading-acting mode, this is not a memorising part, in that there should not be attempts to disguise the fact he is reading direct from the page. Indeed, the fact that he is in reality reading from his 'report' is part of the play.

Act 1
1.

(Lighting up as, initially, back lighting to the back drop's Goddess form and as spot emerges on READER SMITH at front stage.

NOTE: READER SMITH always addresses the audience as though he sees it collectively as being his wife Helen.)

READER SMITH: Helen, I tried my best to put it all down for you. You'll have to give me that. But, you know, the plain truth is my senses scream every time I sat down to try.
(pause)
But then, I had to keep remembering we have most times given each other only pain and, if I stopped, it would only be through a cowardice I never showed before when it came to hurting you, right?
(and)
Then again, too, maybe, just maybe, I might have gotten to write a bit of the pain out for us both. I dunno. I guess what I can't promise is salve. But, as you know, the conversations in my head always begin to take over. All those mad inner rehearsals, you know? Set pieces. So, in trying to get all this down for you, I decided to call myself Smith.
(pause)
I said Smith. Plain and simple Smith. That's me.
(and)
Why not? I've never felt I could rub two pennies together by being myself, so when I was trying to give a name to myself, the commonest of monikers feels right. I won't have any trouble from you about *that*.

(The actor SMITH emerges on elevated 'play' level. He has his back to READER SMITH)

READER SMITH: (pointing him out) See. Smith. Here he is. And just so you'll know...
(he turns to SMITH and says to him:)

'I turn to me.'
    (SMITH dutifully turns to him)
'Smith turns away from me.'
    (SMITH does so)
'He turns back to he-as-me.'

SMITH: (annoyed) What's doing?

READER SMITH: Don't tell me I'm getting a bit cheesed off
with me?

SMITH: You whacked?

READER SMITH: (back to audience/Helen) So, if you don't
mind, Helen, when I read 'Smith' know I'm trying to talk about
me really and when I say 'me' I talking about me'n'Smith, 'kay?
Think of it as a case of you blow, I torch.
    (then)
So if we've got that down pat...

(He takes up the written sheets he will read from and:)

READER SMITH: Okay, so here's Smith finally got to India, and
here's trying to set the scene for you...
    (begins reading from his writings)
'This Kerala. This India. The government says ten million,
conservative, baby girls murdered in the last ten years at birth.
Well, they don't say 'murder'. 'Discrepancies' they register them
as. But, okay, that's the great nation of India's business. Okay,
but smoking a little hash or whatever with a whacked-out looney
of a wise man and maybe being a little dopey for thinking he could
change things that've been going on for centuries... you tell me
what was in any of that to get our boy treated like that?'
    (but stops for a moment for:)
Helen, look... just don't let it get you crazy, okay? Just let it be
me being the coward and telling you what happened by writing,
rather than fronting you face-to-face. Okay? Okay?...
    (has to stop for a moment)
Our boy, once. Our Terry. Remember? Remember.

8

(Indian street background sounds emerge. For a moment there is an explosion of this and then, as if the senses have gotten used to it, it subsides. SMITH, the actor, is momentarily thrown off by the confusion the street sounds represent. He is hurt by dwelling on thinking of his son.

READER SMITH uses his spot to highlight SMITH's discomfort while his own voice is emotionally charged as he begins reading again:)

READER SMITH: 'Smith was filled with something approaching real dread that he might have arrived at the dead end of the world, rather than the dead end of a street in a small town in southwest India. Here was the place of our Terry's passing yet he was surrounded... he was being pushed around... by shove-forms. How could all this seeming chaos bring a learning of what had happened? The thought kept re-occurring: amongst all this, how could one death of one child be even registered against all this utter annihilation to us all, as it looked like just then...?
    (then)
Smith could've cried out for the impossibility of ever being able to find the soul of our Terry in this half-world of grievous wanderings. Such horror did he feel.'

(During this, SINGH has appeared in his doorway of the Singh Boarding House. It is obviously beneath a sign for an ultra-sound baby clinic, even though it is situated next door. The doctor's glasses flash in the light as though over-here Morse code.

SMITH appears to have to struggle against a tide of people and vehicles to cross over to him)

SMITH: Dr Singh?

SINGH: (nodding) My wife and I will help you with your son, Mr Smith.

SMITH: Good to meet you.

9

SINGH: It is, it is.

(SMITH indicates the fertility clinic sign)

SMITH: Am I sharing a room with an up'n'coming mum?

SINGH: No, no. Hello?
    (indicating sign)
Next door, Mr Smith.

SMITH: Yours?

SINGH: (proud, nodding) We have just introduced a new
machine, Mr Smith.
    (reading sales info in his mind)
'The GE Voluson 730 is a 3D/4D ultrasound with the ability to
create volumetric images.'

SMITH: That sounds interesting.

SINGH: It is a very interesting brochure.

(SMITH gazes up at the sign above his head for a little too
long, and:)

SINGH: Are you actually reading what we are saying, Mr Smith?

SMITH: Sorry.

SINGH: No, no. Hello? Do you think you could read it out aloud
while you're at it?

SMITH: (confused) When I said 'sorry', I meant looking at it for
too long... or something.

SINGH: Sorry, sorry. It's just that we'd like to hear what it says
from, don't you know?, the reading public's point of view.

SMITH: (very doubtfully) Okay...

SINGH: Hello?, I mean we don't get much of a chance to canvas public opinion in the home-grown business.

SMITH: I guess not.

(He goes to make a move to go inside the boarding house but SINGH doesn't budge as he waits for SMITH....)

SMITH: Oh, you mean it, ha ha...?

(He points confirmation up at sign)

SINGH: If you'll be so kind, Mr Smith.

(However silly he feels, SMITH does as he is requested. When he reads the sign out aloud, READER SMITH joins in with him and sprays the sign with his spot as though it was in neon:)

SMITH and READER SMITH: 'Don't swell up disappointed. Populations controlled; proven gynaecological menus in range. Open 7 days 3 pm almost. Husbands welcome. Dr J. J. J. Singh, MD (Mumbai), Gynaecologist and Coroner. Viagra discounts.'

(SMITH tries flippancy on a very appreciative SINGH)

SMITH: Abortions, you think?

SINGH: (very serious) In a way.

SMITH: You're talking *your* abortions?

SINGH: In a way.
    (urbanely, introducing himself again)
Mr Smith, I presume.

SMITH: (thinking it a joke again) Dr Singh in a way?
    (but can't let the sign 'go')
'Gynaecological menus'...?

11

SINGH: Hello?, small interventions at the fork of life's road, Mr Smith, ha ha.

SMITH: 'Gynaecologist and Coroner'?

SINGH: The Singh with the 'J. J. J.', hello?

SMITH: That's pretty impressive, all those 'j's.
   (looking around)
And I noticed you said 'we'.

SINGH: (sagely) Mrs Singh is always listening, you know.

SMITH: I see. Well, listen, thanks for offering to help.

SINGH: Ah, there you see... Mrs Singh, my wife, always says an empty promise keeps the empty guest bed away, ha ha.

SMITH: (desperation) Look, I'm pretty tired. Do you think I might come in?

> *(But this corresponds with obviously a couple of buses thundering past with horns blaring. SMITH has to give up, just wait)*

SMITH: Sorry, did you say something?

SINGH: Pardon?

SMITH: (indicating buses) Were you trying to say something?

SINGH: In India, that is often a blessing, no?

SMITH: (his turn) Pardon?

SINGH: Trying to say something. In India, we are generally pretty good at that our words not reaching the ears, you see. But, my dear man, don't just stand there. I know how trying our streets are. Come in and meet my Number One, my dear wife. Mrs

Singh boasts as being the moistest of a hostess, ha ha. My dear wife will make your eyes water, don't you know.

SMITH: Do you think I could get past?

(SINGH realises he is blocking the way, steps aside)

SINGH: Sorry, sorry.

SMITH: No, I'm sorry. Sorry.

(SINGH ushers him inside as the lighting fades from them.

It is only a small blackout.

When a stage area light comes back on gradually, the prop is the end of a dining table. As LAKSHMI SINGH emerges into view in all her splendour, READER SMITH plays his light on her, narrates from the page:)

READER SMITH: 'Lakshmi Singh, oh yes. I tell you, Helen, she was dressed only in a work-a-day salwar – or at least, Smith presumed -- yet she still seemed to be glisteningly decked out. Her face shined with eye-attention as though she was on a silent movie set. Even at first sight she exuded an energy that seemed in spite of her size. And the other thing was she was somehow greeting Smith with all grace and all attention without missing a beat of laying out the table for a cup of tea, which she forgot to give him anyway. She was a performance already started, like as if you were late and she was already in a dance that must rise above your late entry. Her heavy thighs thumped on the Kashmir rug, gave tremors to the floor, even if it was polished concrete under the mats...'

(By now she is in full view and full flight)

LAKSHMI: Mr Smith! Entrez!

SINGH: (cautionary) He is very tired, my dear, hello?

LAKSHMI: I am not going to smother him, Dr Singh. Take no notice of my silly old hubby, Mr Smith! Welcome, welcome, to our Indian specials of tea with its three quarters of Indian squeezed-out milk and semolina shortbreads the like of which have not seen better ghee. Not in the Australian Outback, anyway. Your first Indian holiday tale to tell sitting around the camp fire, Mr Smith!

SMITH: I'll certainly keep it in mind.

LAKSHMI: Mr Smith. Mr Smith. Sit. Sit. Stand. Stand but do it comfortably, Mr Smith.

> *(She stops fussing around to stand before SMITH in a histrionic theatrical pose, even with fingertip coquettishly beneath her chin. She examines him up and down.*
>
> *A small shiver expresses her disappointment at what she sees before taking SMITH by the hand and pumping it madly while she bursts into a Bharatanatyam sequence in the half-sitting position, nearly pulling him off his feet)*

SINGH: Hello?, Mr Smith, Mrs Singh is a mistress of Bharatanatyam,

SMITH: (out of ignorance) Lucky joe, Bharatanatyam.

> *(She gives him a playful punch on the shoulder which nearly knocks him over)*

LAKSHMI: Oh, you two big kidders! Bharatanatyam is the local dancings, Mr Smith.

SMITH: (doesn't) I know.

LAKSHMI: (stopping in disbelief) But Bharatanatyam is a Hindi word, Mr Smith made for Hindus.

SMITH: (trying to get out of it) I just know it... sort of.

(She stops to examine if he is being ridiculous or serious.

Finally, she decides he is neither – but rather a willing audience -- and performs for him a small burst of a series of steps, or adavus, and flourishing hastas, or hand movements. After she completes this, she naturally stops in a pose that allows plenty of time for a running commentary of correct appreciation:)

READER SMITH: 'And Bharatanatyam she was. Eyelashed puppetry. It was like she was watching herself dancing the eternal dramas and couldn't wait for those black-liner eyes to express the surprise of being able to do it at all. If I am right there, Lakshmi Singh just had to be the gossip-incarnate eye queen of them all. Her eyelashes were proscenium curtains. Her gold-bangling ears always seemed cocked for sounds coming from beyond whatever set she imagined she was on. She looked like no sound would be too small -- the tinier, the more in tune to it she might be. Her mascara was pure Buster Keaton, and Smith had the impression he might just be hanging from the nearest clock tower.'

LAKSHMI: (not a little pantingly) Yes, very pleased to meet you too, Mr Smith. It is okeydokey to kiss my hand but do not let Dr Singh here stop you going to your room and washing all you want, Mr Smith. Foreigners get terrifically smelly here at this time of year. You'll be glad to know that our people think Germans are the worse from wear and tear and Australians are well down the list. They say the armpits of Germany are made from the pits upwards. You poor smelling man you, you will find there is no cleanser like Indian water applied generously to secret parts.

(She somehow pulls a towel and a cake of soap from her salvar, pushes them onto him, then beckons for him to follow)

LAKSHMI: Prepare yourself for bed, Mr Smith, on the back of the time warp coming from Australia gives.

(She drags SMITH off. SINGH follows.

Blackout in that area, while READER SMITH returns to his spot.

As he speaks, LAKSHMI re-emerges to stand under his spotlight, happily giving herself up for inspection again)

READER SMITH: 'Helen, I know this's got nothing to do with anything, but I have to try to nail her down. I mean, surely there couldn't be anyone more Indian in Mrs Lakshmi Singh than her size. If broad is as a boab tree's bum, she's as Indian as scarified butter. Her body had to be a larder for it, the ghee part of tea-and-ghee. She moved as stunningly blancmange, as decorously of nates, as hindmost parading, as the Lord Shiva's sacred bull would have had His oestrous herd do. All the way upstairs to show him his room, her eyes had not stopped rolling, perhaps in an imagery of nosing up to a German armpit or just in a perpetual Lord Shiva at bounce and twirl. Smith could see how she must be immensely sexually exciting if you thrill to the soft and buttery, or being externally absorbed. He couldn't help himself thinking like that; you know what he's like, Helen.'

> *(LAKSHMI moves from the 'inspection', busies herself to making up what has now become a bed form and its surrounds...)*

LAKSHMI: Honesty, you Australians. Bed is all you think about, isn't it so, Dr Singh?

SINGH: (appalled at her again) Hello, hello?

> *(Of course she ignores him, but kindly)*

LAKSHMI: Mr Smith, they say people from that uggers country called Pakistani are the worst when it comes to spittle over women folk where the mouth waters, but don't quote me on that unless it's true or unless you didn't hear it here first.

SMITH: (ignorantly) Sorry if I offended.

LAKSHMI: Please don't offend in these premises, Mr Smith.

SMITH: I didn't mean...

SINGH: (to help him out) Hello?, nobody will ever find a piece of meat like Mrs Lakshmi Singh on any one of my mortuary tables, Mr Smith, ha ha.

SMITH: I bet.

LAKSHMI: (seriously curious) Bet what?

SMITH: (quickly) That's not meant as an offense.

LAKSHMI: Pardon piggy?

SMITH: Betting. No offense.

LAKSHMI: (to her husband) Dr Singh, show Mr Smith where the bookmaker plies his offensive trade.

SINGH: Hello?, Mr Smith doesn't want the bookmaker, my dear.

LAKSHMI: You are not to take bettings in these premises, Dr Singh.

SINGH: Never, my dear.

LAKSHMI: (re-assured) One can never be too careful, Mr Smith. Indian husbands don't come in with the cows, you know.

SINGH: Hello, hello...?

(She has finished with the bed, gets down to business)

LAKSHMI: (hearkening up) And make your first stop first up of all before anything, Mr Smith.
(to his silent query)
I am talking of the morgue, where I have never been near, which is near the hospital vicinities going through its front door after going out of ours here. There, you will find your dear son's body

17

where it should not be. But first, bathe, Mr Smith. Under the armpits do it well. Then go and identify your poor dear Terry. Then you come right back here for tea with milk sugar, take it from me, where we have even more help to be served up.

DR SINGH: (it's his domain) Hello?, hello?, my dear...

LAKSHMI: (waving him off) Hello, hello, yourself, Dr Singh! I will be available later at any time as of now, Mr Smith. My husband hereabouts, who will try to busy himself sillily, you betcha, if you don't insist on his going with you, has arranged for that distasteful policeman fellow named Lingayya to be at the morgue when you might arrive if you follow our directions carefully. It is with regret I am unable to find out about the passage of bodies from India to Australia since it might also be useful for future guests. However, I can recommend our local fires, Mr Smith. We are a religious people who have had many terrific years in having good send-offs with fires using local wood. We Indians say tenderer and tinderer, ha ha. Don't noggin me, you two silly men, only a niggle'll do. I am only thinking of your dear dead boy Terry lying all alone out there.

(She dabs her eyes, and her tears are genuine)

SMITH: This police guy... Lingayya?... he knows what happened to Terry?

LAKSHMI: Him? He would not tell a rooster from a rotten egg...
    (stops to think, then:)
Do you think I might have coined that first ever, Mr Smith?

SMITH: Good chance, I'd say.

LAKSHMI: (quoting herself with relish) '... rooster from a rotten egg'
    (and)
Then kindly remember, you heard it first within these four walls, Mr Smith. And call me Lakshmi or don't call me when you need me, ha ha.

SMITH: (obediently) Lakshmi.

LAKSHMI: It's a terribly good Indian name, Mr Smith.

SMITH: I know.

LAKSHMI: It's so good to have tourists who do their homework first, Mr Smith!

> *(She dusts off her hand having finished his room and then, quite alarmingly, as if in some Hollywood gangster role:)*

LAKSHMI: ('that's-it-then') 'Kay. You hip, then, Smithee?

SINGH: (appalled at her again) Hello? Hello?

LAKSHMI: (but in full flight) I cannot find out about what happened to your son, Mr Smith. Indian people, you know, tight along the lips. I will try my best, and call me look-out-Madam Mountain-coming-through when it comes to that. Let me tell you, though, the first visit-over after your first visit-over to the morgue should be to the village where your son stayed instead of here as we strongly advised. But first have your good trip to the morgue, Mr Smith.

> *(She launches herself conspiratorially at SMITH, who is so alarmed he cannot avoid her)*

LAKSHMI: But let me tell you first before even that, Mr Smith, there is very much in nature that is evil about that village I just mentioned. Ssh. Enough said for now, so keep it zipped for now, you naughty impatient old thing, you.

> *(Lights begin to fade, with SMITH is real danger of being bodily absorbed by her, and as she:)*

LAKSHMI: But!

SMITH: (startled) But what?

SINGH: (equally so too) What?

LAKSHMI: But your poor dear son Terrence should not have stayed in that village while we had terrific off-season rates here, Mr Smith.

SMITH: (almost outcry) I'm sorry!

LAKSHMI: I would have warned him about wandering in the nights during Indian darkness where there is a marked difference between what can be seen and what cannot be copped-a-gander-at. Not to mention... so kindly don't... warning him to stay away from the dirty priest they call Nandi Baba. What a dirty priest! Please, Mr Smith, the same goes for you with bells on.
    (grabbing him alarmingly again)
See your poor dear son, then go home.

SINGH: (enough's enough) Hello, my dear? Forget the name Nandi Baba, Mr Smith. Hello?

LAKSHMI: (greater warning) Go home, Mr Smith. Look to correcting your country's immigration policy drowning little children at sea. Occupy yourself well.

(While scene fades, SMITH breaks off from them)

SMITH: (into air) Nandi Baba. That fucking maniac.

(Blackout)

2.

(Sounds rise of the town – the traffic, the shop music, the people bustle.

These sound levels rise and modulate until they fade into wind in trees and crows crying over empty land, giving the impression of a small journey across town SMITH has gone on.

READER SMITH will use his spot to 'travel' with SMITH as he goes. Then fuller lighting will come up on the bleak morgue area....)

READER SMITH: 'I tell you, Helen, Smith had never been as spooked as he was when he approached that morgue. It was at the back of the local hospital... basically a tin shed in a clearing that wasn't much of a clearing anymore. At least the sumptuous Lakshmi Singh had been right about that prick of a copper, Lingayya, would be waiting.'

(Lighting up on LINGAYYA tapping his lathi impatiently and menacingly on his thigh in a very bleak area of the stage)

SINGH: (sotto voce) Be careful with this one, Mr Smith.

SMITH: Why, doesn't that dopey moustache tickle?

SINGH: He is said to be full of blind fury.

(They proceed onto LINGAYYA who acknowledges their approach with very menacing lathi thigh-slapping)

SMITH: You tap-tap me with that stick thing and I'll tap-tap you, how's that?

LINGAYYA: (at SINGH) Is this the one?

(Getting a cautious nod, LINGAYYA leers unpleasantly at SMITH, then turns and walks off, expecting the others to follow)

SINGH: Hello?, Mr Smith. You are expected to follow him.

SMITH: Where?

SINGH: Into the morgue.

SMITH: That's the morgue? What does it do, double as a garage?

SINGH: (shrugging apologetically) It's really all on the basis of complaints, you see. There's not many complaints.

SMITH: It's a morgue full of the... morgue'd. Who's going to complain?

SINGH: ('logic') That's why that's the morgue, dear fellow.

SMITH: Oh, right, and that's why there's no complaints about it

SINGH: Exactly.
     (pointing after LINGAYYA)
Hello?, we really ought to catch up.

SMITH: We're not going to get any help from that prick. We already hate each other.

SINGH: Without him we don't see any dead person, you see. It's the law.

SMITH: Up his. Why... what is he...?

SINGH: We really ought to be going. Inspector. Acting, I think, you see.

SMITH: Why someone here so high as an Inspector?

SINGH: I don't know, Mr Smith.

SMITH: I have to ask Mrs Singh?

SINGH: Hello?! I think it is something about him being one of the last people to see your son, you see.

SMITH: See my son how?

LINGAYYA: (shouting back) You pissers coming or not?

(SINGH immediately hurries to catch up. It leaves SMITH with no alternative but to do the same.

Blackout)

3.

(Spot on intimations of a disgraceful morgue interior.

It is so gloomy in there that the figures of SMITH, SINGH and LINGAYYA actually emerge into sight, while:)

READER SMITH: 'They went through a curtain of flies rather than a door. Inside, there was none of smell of disinfectant Smith was expecting but only a sort of heavy, unmoved mugginess. That air was sweaty and fetid, and that, together with the real-or-imagined rotting flesh from the engine-drones of all those flies, made Smith think of an abattoir. When his sight got used to the light, on the far wall cascaded what looked like splattered dried blood. It spread down to and then along the broken concrete floor. Its bright red splatter looked bloody spurtings out of jugulars or something and evoked a violence done to our Terry that brought vomit to Smith's throat, his hand to the doctor's arm... The tap-tapping of that damn lathi...'

LINGAYYA: Get on with it.

SINGH: (to SMITH re wall stains) Hello?, it's only betel juice they spit out, Mr Smith, not blood, but what to do?

SMITH: Didn't you say this is your place?

SINGH: I am the Chief Pathologist as well, yes, but sadly very restricted.

23

SMITH: Who's your boss? Who do I see?

SINGH: The Coroner.

SMITH: You're the Coroner!

SINGH: I am, I am.

> *(but there doesn't seem anymore to say on the matter)*

LINGAYYA: I said get on with it.

SMITH: (still at SINGH) You didn't do... anything to Terry and then go spitting against the wall?

SINGH: (choosing words) I don't spit against the walls.

> *(LINGAYYA taps the ground at SMITH's feet)*

LINGAYYA: Hey, foreigner. You blind?

> *(It makes SMITH actually get ready for a fight)*

SMITH: *What*?

SINGH: The Inspector is sadly meaning don't move and look down, Mr Smith, before you accidentally trip over something.

> *(The prop has turned into what looks like a covered stretcher on a slab. SMITH pulls away from walking into it)*

SINGH: Hello?, I only say that because it would be terrible form for you to fall over your poor Terry, Mr Smith.

> *(LINGAYYA sniggers)*

SINGH: (great embarrassment) Please don't mind the cracks around the edges, we actually did find a spare dissecting table for

24

you to inspect the young man on, Mr Smith. I can assure you that anything which leaks from it runs down along these channels here and into the drain you might see running out into the garden where our most luxurious flowers are.

(SMITH still can't make out what the covered stretcher is)

SMITH: What is it?

LINGAYYA: Right, this your son or not?'

(He rips back the cover from the stretcher.

READER SMITH sprays his light on the stretcher for a moment as SMITH leans over his son.

He turns light off quickly. Can only turn and stare at the audience just as SMITH can only stare down at the stretcher. Finally:)

SMITH: (absolutely dully) What he doing on a camp stretcher?

(There is only a LINGAYYA's snigger as answer.

Blackout)

4.

(In this lighting interim, we hear SMITH saying dully again, 'What's he doing on a camp stretcher?'

READER SMITH switches back on his spot but merely has to play on his own feet such that he is barely visible to the audience. He is staring out at them... the stunned and grieved look on his face reflecting the deadness in SMITH's voice.

Eventually, READER SMITH gets himself to start up again...)

READER SMITH: 'Helen, listen. Listen. Listen. Listen. Listen. Listen... That stretcher was where they had dumped our Terry. Dumped. Dumped, you see. I...

(He barely forces himself back to the pages. His reading is staccato and eerie in the semi-darkness:)

READER SMITH: A dirtied-canvas stretcher from... what?, where? Where did they get such a thing? With rusted iron supports. Beneath a torn and soiled sheet. Maybe not even a sheet. A piece of filthy cloth. Something crude and ragged. Something left over. Filthy. On a filthy cement slab they used to cut them up. Dead meat. Discarded. Smith heard someone groan, but it might have been himself. Smith saw someone go forward to the stretcher. But I think he might have been somehow watching himself.

(Lighting returns to the play area. SMITH has not moved from the stretcher. His eventual cry is some cri de coeur.)

SMITH: *What is he doing on a camp stretcher?*

SINGH: (displacement apology) They do not make real canvas like that anymore, Mr Smith.

SMITH: *What?*

SINGH: (greatly apologetic) It's the best stretcher that money can buy. Well, you can't buy it any more...

(has to trail off)

LINGAYYA: (at SINGH) Get him to get a move on.

SINGH: Hello?, easy on, Inspector.

LINGAYYA: (to SMITH, viciously) You should have got here sooner, *puta*.

SMITH: (swinging around) What did this prickhead say?

LINGAYYA: I take that as a yes. Get him to put acceptance in writing to me.

> *(With a final and loud snigger down at SMITH, he walks out.*
>
> *SINGH reaches out to touch SMITH)*

SINGH: Mr Smith, Smithee...?

> *(SMITH simply collapses to sit on the floor with his back to the dissecting table)*

SINGH: I wouldn't be sitting down there, don't you know, Mr Smith.

SMITH: (dully) Why?

SINGH: We are still trying very, very hard to persuade a certain cobra to take up a new home.

SMITH: I'm not asking about any cobra.

SINGH: Oh, sorry.
  (tries beefing up conversation)
Well, hello?, as we were saying, I believe that stretcher came in the Great War. Wonderful bit of Allied field equipment, that.

SMITH: I'm not asking about any fucking stretcher.

> *(SMITH waves that off, reaches up to tap the body)*

SMITH: *Fucking why, fucking why?*

SINGH: Oh, sorry. From a medical point of view...

SMITH: (cutting him off) There's something about the eyes. Mouth, or something. *I can't see!*

SINGH: (alarmed for him, kindly) Hello, hello?, Mr Smith. You're talking about the empty sockets and, regrettably, the loss of lips. Please believe me, it's not uncommon. It's nothing personal.

READER SMITH: (butting in with his own outcry) 'Sockets! Caves of chalk! Eye-less! Listen, listen, lid-less, lip-less! God help me, Helen, the holes of taxidermy!'

SMITH: *That's my boy there*!

SINGH: (sinking into professionalism) And a natural reaction, Mr Smith. Hello?, regrettably, one has to lay it at the feet of the crows and mices.

SMITH: *Mices*?

SINGH: ('definitely') Mices. You see, they tend to run riot in our poor morgue, don't you know. Pitter patter, pitter patter. No that one would want anyone to feel comfortable lying here. Still, at least with the crows and the mices you can discount the possibility of some criminal trade going on with any trade in eyes, yes?, no? And one could admit we could do with a few more facilities. You know, we did have a dissecting table that swivelled, but it just stopped swivelling. We do have terrific storage units over there, but they get a bit overheated in there without electricity. The electricity only awaits for the air conditioning machines to come but they are not coming without the electricity. It's all a question of engineering, way over my head, Mr Smith. Hello?, and as you can see, with the lighting system one would not know which end is up and which end is down which often cause many a slip between cut and lip.
    (and)
Actually, if we'd known you were coming a bit sooner we might have managed a bit of spring cleaning. But you can't believe how

hard scrubbing brushes are to get under budgetary constraints, you know.
(and)
Mr Smith, hello?, come any given morning one has to expect the crows and the mices to hop onboard any eyes lying around. They prize eyes. I don't know what that means zoologically.

SMITH: Are you being funny?

SINGH: What do you mean?

(SMITH gets to his feet aggressively)

SMITH: My Terry's been picked *clean*!

SINGH: Ah, as for that, that's the cockroaches' fault, of course. We block off the front door but it's the holes in the walls. Still, a terrifically persistent thing, Nature, isn't it? There is a saying that our cockroaches have the sharpest teeth in India, don't you know.

SMITH: I'm not signing for my boy like that.

SINGH: Are you sure?

SMITH: I'M NOT SIGNING FOR MY BOY LIKE THAT!

SINGH: (the reasonable man again) Mr Smith, who would in that condition? Not I.

SMITH: Oh, God. Oh, God.
(He lurches out.

Blackout)

5.

READER SMITH: (himself recovering) 'There was defeat here for Smith. Truth be known, he was actually feeling just bone tired. Can you remember, Helen?... you know, how you go to India and you get on their wheel of existence and you know by the way your head starts turn-turning why they have come to believe in it. At least it's something going in some direction and quite possibly getting you on the way to somewhere even if it is around in circles.'

(Lighting up on LAKSHMI SINGH in full flight and fussing towards SMITH)

LAKSHMI: (tearfully in sympathy) Mr Smith, I hope I have come up with, or is it to?, the goods. But first, none of this is for publication please. The village your poor Terrence stayed at is called Manvoor, just across the sun drenched waters we are rightly famous for in photographs. I do not know why he took up residencies there when you take into account our clean sheets. I need say no more. So, Mr Smith, this is what I have dug up. Are we ready or not? Tomorrow morning, my husband, Dr Singh, has been persuaded by these lips to take you over there. You will see an evil priest called Nandi Baba... priest?, pull this one, buster! Beware Nandi Baba, Mr Smith. This will be after breakfast, then you should have your loins gilded, wet and wiped and ready to choof off to Manvoor, hasta la vista, baby...

(She literally push-shoves-places him on the prop which is now his bed. He sits abjectly. She takes him head and pulls it into her ample stomach. He doesn't resist)

LAKSHMI: Dear Mr Smith, don't you drop your Aussie bundle. Yerk on what it might contain foreign to us locals if Mad Max is to be believed. But if Dr Singh was here...

SINGH: (appearing) Hello?, I am, my dear.

LAKSHMI: (accusing him) I don't know what you did to this poor man.

SINGH: I did nothing, my dear!

LAKSHMI: Did you show him his poor Terry?

SINGH: Hello?, they had even brought him inside and placed him on the old stretcher. You remember the old canvas stretcher, Mrs Singh?

LAKSHMI: (sagely) I do, I do.
  (then)
Did you want something, Dr Singh?

SINGH: No, my dear.

LAKSHMI: Are you thinking of interfering with what is my turn now?

SINGH: Never!

    (He hurriedly departs.

    She lifts SMITH's face to look into hers)

LAKSHMI: You must be forgiving what that naughty man did, Mr Smith. He did not take the Indian Tourist Bureau's course like I did. You go ahead, kid, and just tell me what you are dying to tell me.

    (She is right; SMITH does want to 'confess'. He speaks up to her, but it is very leaden:)

SMITH: My wife's name is Helen... well, she in Sri Lanka, me in Melbourne...

LAKSHMI: Send her an all-paid airline ticket to Melbourne, Mr Smith.

SMITH: It's gone way further than that.

LAKSHMI: (with much insight) You may call me as if I am Helen, Mr Smith...

SMITH: (unabashed to do so) Helen.

LAKSHMI: Hmm?

SMITH: No, see, what I was going to say to you, Helen, was...

(READER SMITH suddenly appears in his own spot and joins in with him:)

SMITH and READER SMITH: ... was that right from the start you and I got giddy too when we went there to adopt the twins. You remember how excited we were, waiting for them in that hole of a room they made us wait in, and then our confusion, then fury, when they brought in only little Terry and not the little baby girl?... and Smith stupidly piping up, 'Hey, we've paid for two!' and you holding Terry like they might snatch him back as well, and Smith starting shouting we want our little Louise too, because we had already named her, she was already ours...? God almighty. Remember how that whole so-called adoption agency had gone empty all of a sudden? You remember screeching? You remember those Indian cops, smirking away with one message for us. Take the baby boy and count your lucky stars, or leave empty handed and kiss all your money goodbye, you rich turds...?

(READER SMITH fades out. SMITH grabs LAKSHMI's hand)

SMITH: We had named her Louise before we met her but then we left her behind. How could we do that?

LAKSHMI: Never you mind that now.

SMITH: And now the boy.

LAKSHMI: You are drops in their ocean, Mr Smith.

SMITH: Yes.

32

LAKSHMI: Go to Manvoor village and then take your Terry home.

SMITH: Not until I know.

LAKSHMI: Know what, Mr Smith?

SMITH: *I don't know*!

LAKSHMI: Oh, you poor man!

(Blackout)

6.

(Through a darkened stage, READER SMITH, LAKSHMI and SINGH appear in spots in their respective areas)

READER SMITH: It was a forty-minute ferry trip over to the village side. You didn't have to be less bone tired than Smith to expect at any moment all the lagoon's dykes, all the rotted-toothed fishing settlements perched on ground barely above the dense currents, to collapse under the sheer threat of mudslide...'

LAKSHMI: (piping up) They have bodies floating away down our waterways that are never seen in any or our brochures, Mr Smith. Do not under any craving drink the water.

READER SMITH: 'She said.'

LAKSHMI: You heard it first from this humble Indian housewife, Mr Smith.

READER SMITH: 'She said. But what was Terry doing shifting over and staying on the other ferry side from the town?'

LAKSHMI: Mr Smith, while you are over in that evil side, watch where your toes are pointing at all times.

READER SMITH: 'She said. And I said, "Mrs Singh, you are fussing".'

LAKSHMI: Washing awaits your socks when you return, Mr Smith.

SINGH: Hello, hello? We must be going.

LAKSHMI: Don't be a pot with such fuss, Dr Singh.

(Return to blackout)

7.

('Water-way' lighting and sounds softly.

Then the looming shape is illuminated as the fearsome Kali Chinnamasta. She has bloodshot eyes and a bloodied, protruding tongue. Her four hag arms seemed frozen in the middle of a mad fit; her pubic mound enormous. Around her neck she sports a necklace of skulls, which hung down past her knees; in her lower left hand she carries a screaming human head, over which her curved mouth is in constant ridicule of the mortal pain she is inflicting.

SMITH and SINGH come together.

They are outside a convent, where there is a small platform of sorts cemented onto the outside walls near the main gates.

A figure hangs back in the shadows.)

SMITH: (up a statue) Charming.

SINGH: (very uneasily) Kali Chinnamasta.

SMITH: This one feed on people or something?

SINGH: Kali Chinnamasta feeds on babies. Hello?, mainly unwanted babies.

SMITH: Yeah, and mainly little girls, right?

(SINGH is uncomfortable talking about this. Finally:)

SINGH: Some little boys too.

SMITH: Like crippled ones. Useless ones. The ones like girls, not wanted.

SINGH: How else can the Goddess take away their sins?

SMITH: You mean the parents?

SINGH: Them too.

(He is fearing of the statue nonetheless)

SINGH: Don't look at it too long, Mr Smith. Hello?

SMITH: So much for India fighting off the corrupting influence of McDonald's.

SINGH: Hello?, there is a Christian shrine to the Crossroads Mother Mary. Actually, you are standing on it, and I do wish you wouldn't, Mr Smith.

(SMITH steps away quickly from an ornamented rock on the ground)

SMITH: Shit, it's nowhere near the cross roads.

(SINGH indicates the convent doors)

SINGH: Aha, it would be if it wasn't very much downhill when it rains, aitcha?

SMITH: That's a rock.

SINGH: Hello?, an important rock. With paint. Gloss if I'm not mistaken. A popular coating around here for important shrines.
    (offering)
Do you want a picture of it?

SMITH: I only want this Nandi Baba guy.

        (SMITH looks around further afield)

SMITH: So this it? Into the village Mrs Singh said and out the other side?

        (SINGH nods, points to a place on a very basic map the other is holding)

SINGH: Here.
    (exceedingly proudly)
You know, as Mrs Singh says, our humble boarding house is the only place in the world where you wouldn't be charged for a map like this, hello?, Mr Smith.

SMITH: (simple observation) It's in Russian.

SINGH: And very reflective of our region's heady tourist aims.

SMITH: Right, but first they should maybe think of
    (sweeping hand around)
cleaning up the joint. There's nothing wrong with mangrove swamps that prohibiting it from being a rubbish dump wouldn't fix.

SINGH: Household waste does help to snag unwanted things floating off into the sea before we can park our noses into it, don't you know.

SMITH: Well, 'kay, you've brought me here. We've been through the 'evil' Manvoor as Mrs Singh called it.

SINGH: Splendid woman.

SMITH: Ain't that a fact.
    (looking)
Lady of Fatima Convent...?

SINGH: (as though to a child) Right here.

SMITH: I know it's right here, Doctor. Why's it right here?

SINGH: Well, it's outside of the town which is very good for a Christian religion, you know.

    (SMITH gives up, indicates the crib affair attached to the convent wall)

SMITH: What's this crib-thing for?

SINGH: Hello? You can put your unwanted baby there, usually after dark, isn't it? It saves me a lot of work as Coroner but it is not so good for the fertility clinic, no?

SMITH: What do they do with them?

SINGH: Don't worry. I'm sure they don't do what they might have done to your Louise, Mr Smith.
    (SMITH turns sharply to him)
Regrettably I heard you talking to Mrs Singh. I'm sure she didn't end up on the streets of Calcutta or something like most of the orphans snatched in those adoption rackets that happened to you.
    (then)
Hello?, please forget I said anything.

SMITH: (finally) I asked.
    (pause)
We seeing this Nandi Baba priest guy in there? He Catholic?

SINGH: Good Lord, I wouldn't have thought so.
   (draws closer for just-between-the-two-of-us)
The Baba is a Kapalika, a madness sect, Mr Smith.

SMITH: Sound interesting.

SINGH: No, it is not, of course. They walk around with a human skull for their begging bowl. They smear themselves with the ashes of the dead. They are called The Left-Handers, got from the left hand tantras.

SMITH: What do they go in for?

SINGH: Hello?, madness, shouting and cursing. Chaos, Mr Smith. They make virtues to Lord Shiva of blood and alcohol and meat and sexual fluids. They walk about, walk into places, screaming blue murder and swearing a lot with their snakes and mongrel street dogs. They will shout and say they're going to kill you. It's from the wrath of their lord Bhairava, the aspect of Lord Shiva who sprang into life in rage over his brother Brahma's constant boasting and cut off one of His five heads. Because of that He had to wander the earth with that skull stuck to his palm, don't you know.

SMITH: A bit of trouble on the wheel rim, eh?

SINGH: I don't think I understand.

SMITH: ('never mind') So is this Nandi Baba really a real priest?

SINGH: It is as Mrs Singh said, of course.

SMITH: You know, Doctor, this Hinduism is a real bombs-away.

SINGH: No, no.

SMITH: What's this got to do with...
   (indicating convent)
Rome?

(SINGH points to the baby-receiving crib)

SINGH: This is where your Terry was often seen, you see.

(SMITH goes over to the crib, runs his hands over it, fails to get a feeling of much. Finally:)

SMITH: You brought me here to see this Nandi Baba.

(SINGH nods, points opposite across the track)

SMITH: (confused) Where?

SINGH: There, next to the cemetery.

SMITH: That mud hut?

SINGH: He doesn't wander around too much anymore, Mr Smith. He can't steal to make much money anymore, I suppose. Normally he'd probably have a swimming pool.

SMITH: And has she anything to do with it?

(He points to the figure still lurking in the shadows.

It takes SINGH by surprise, but not the figure. Caught out, pointed out so openly, ANNAPURNA comes out from hiding and blandly walks past them to go off. [She is retreating into NANDI BABA's hut.]

She is wearing a filthy Western floral frock and carrying a wrapped-up six or seven-year-old child, slung from shoulder to hip, very protectively across her chest.)

SINGH: (confused) Hello, hello?

SMITH: Don't ask me. She's been following us since we got off the ferry.

SINGH: I didn't see her.

SMITH: It's pretty dense shitty jungle swampy stuff around here. I thought she was sporting a suicide vest or something. It's a kid.

SINGH: It's a girl about six, they say. Very sick, but she won't let any of us look at the child. They say she never puts the child down.

SMITH: Is she going into the priest's mud hut?

SINGH: She is Nandi Baba's woman.

SMITH: What's that mean?

SINGH: (not a little embarrassed) Woman. Hindu holy men, don't you know. The lingam is always large even if it's only said to be. Hello?, temple dancing girls and all that.

SMITH: That's a dancing girl?

SINGH: (as to an idiot) No, Mr Smith, hardly. They follow them around. They say they know the priest's minds. They talk for them.

SMITH: Her following us is some message or something from the priest?

SINGH: It could be, yes.

> (SMITH suddenly runs after ANNAPURNA)

SMITH: Hey!

> (SINGH is left very uncomfortably standing alone outside the convent.
>
> Light up on the narrator in the meantime)

READER SMITH: 'I can't get out of putting this down, Helen. Her name was Annapurna and this was the first time Smith had

40

laid eyes on her. She was wearing a filthy faded Western floral frock, really stained, as though she had just come from working in a garage. The problem was it was see-through... God help me, I have to tell you all this or nothing at all!... and the other problem was she had her right breast hanging out as though if the child wanted it she could have it immediately. But the problem over all that was Smith knew she knew he couldn't take his eyes off it. No, no, I can't apologise. Somehow that tit was full... mango juicy full... pluckish. As he caught up with her, what with the weight of the child across her front, her bum was grinding hard-pressed glutes. It was! And then at the two sticks in the ground that were supposed to be Nandi Baba's gates, she just sat down and waited for me, for Smith. It was as if Smith had pushed her back onto her back, legs open. I'm sorry, but there it is, warts and all...'

(SMITH finally returns to SINGH, walking rather cramped up, to SINGH)

SMITH: (shrugs) I told her to tell that priest we're coming to see him.

SINGH: (pointing) And from that you achieved a stiffie?
(to SMITH's trying to cover his obvious erection up)
Aitcha, Mrs Singh was right about women only having to snap their fingers under Australian noses.

SMITH: Look, you're a doctor. As soon as I neared her, I couldn't stop it. Me, I'm feeling as sexy as a beach ball, so how does that go?

SINGH: You want some medicine to lower it, Mr Smith? I don't have any on me at the moment.
(pause; genuine scientific inquiry)
Do they?

SMITH: Do who what?

SINGH: Hello?, Australian doctors. Do they have to keep carrying around medicine for that?

41

SMITH: (exasperated) Jesus H.

SINGH: I don't often get consulted on nice problems to have.
   (pointing)
I think the problem is resolving itself anyway...

SMITH: (changing the subject) You said something about Terry
being seen around here a lot. Why was that?

SINGH: (uneasily) Mr Smith, can't you ask Mrs Singh?

SMITH: Can't you just come out with it, man?

SINGH: We ought to be getting on, but someone's wife told
someone who told Mrs Singh that Lingayya's wife told her... for it
probably was a her, don't you know...

SMITH: Wait up. Is that the same Lingayya as that copper with
that lathi thing?

SINGH: Hello?, of course.

SMITH: What's he got to do with it?

SINGH: Well, he's the one who owns the shipping company
where... on the wharf... you know... by his fishing boats, they
found Terry. You know that, Mr Smith, aitcha?

SMITH: Lingayya? Copper and ship owner?

SINGH: Most of the fishing fleet here is his family's, Mr Smith.

SMITH: Isn't anyone what they seem around here?

SINGH: Pardon?

SMITH: (sudden thought) You mean it was his mob who found
Terry that night?

SINGH: That is the thing, I think.

SMITH: So that bully boy could have been one of the last to see him alive?

SINGH: I suppose so, or someone told someone who told someone who told Mrs Singh and, believe me, Mr Smith, Mrs Singh would know.

SMITH: And Terry was beaten real bad, right? You're the Coroner.

SINGH: Regrettably. Mrs Singh was told someone or other might have caught him trespassing among the boats in the middle of the night as he used to go about... we don't know why, hello?... and, well, these things can tragically escalate, don't you know, Mr Smith.

SMITH: I want to see that Lingayya again!

SINGH: But I think if you ask Mrs Singh he has already given you an appointment to meet him at his home. A mansion, really, hello?

SMITH: (fed up) Shit.
     (then)
Are we going or not?

        (Blackout.

        In the interim, READER SMITH:)

READER SMITH: Okay, so across the way was Nandi Baba's mud hut. It was daubed with ochre-and-white squiggles but the biggest colour was the rust on the tin roof. Not a leaf or outside shade... even the cemetery next door had a few more. Alright, yes, the
     (while slow lighting up...)
woman Annapurna was there sitting against the hut. She kept stroking the child's hair and heaving her into a more protective position across her torso as he approached. Now he could see how

43

the kid was so covered in sweat that had spread through her own dress to her mother's and added to its greasy patches. He had the wild thought the child was actually dead. Yeah, all right, his crutch wasn't by a long shot....'

(SMITH advances leaving SINGH waiting back at the gates.

NANDI BABA appears as, first, a roar from inside the hut, then a white demon that emerges leaping up and down in the doorway in pure comic-book rage.

SMITH holds up his hands to try to placate him, but NANDI BABA begins pelting stones with pathetic force and hopeless inaccuracy. As he does so he punctuates each sling with:)

NANDI BABA: 'Get a-vay! Get a-vay, piss off, NOTHING!

(With all his own pent-up emotions, SMITH raves just as much, begins pelting stones back)

SMITH: BASTARD, WHAT'D YOU DO TO MY BOY?!

NANDI BABA: Ha! You haf no dick to haf a boy!

SMITH: Fatso!

NANDI BABA: NOBODY!

(SMITH has the satisfaction of hearing the old priest yelp from being hit with a stone, stop in his frenzy tracks and hightailed back inside his hut with his arms covering his head against the next flurry.

A long silence, until SINGH calls censorially from the gate)

SINGH: That is a holy man, Mr Smith. Hello?

SMITH: (surlily) Yeah, well, he can't field for nuts

(SMITH proceeds onto ANNAPURNA)

SMITH: Everybody's a third umpire.

ANNAPURNA: (showing her English) Yes.

SMITH: Why were you following us did you say?

ANNAPURNA: (frankly, disarmingly) Because the Baba said we will make love.

(SMITH is not in the least taken aback)

SMITH: Oh yeah. and why would he say that?

ANNAPURNA: Because he says it is time to set me free.

SMITH: You here against your free will?

ANNAPURNA: (shaking head) He saved me, now to set me free.

SMITH: What about the child?

ANNAPURNA: Her too.

SMITH: When? The making love bit.

ANNAPURNA: Oh, that. That is easy. Next full moon.

SMITH: I don't know any full moon. I mightn't be here any next full moon.

ANNAPURNA: Yes, you will, Mr Smith. The Nandi Baba thinks you are a true student of the right path and a worthy mid-off fieldsman. He says long live Shane Warne in the universal scheme of things and please do and don't come again. Anytime. Bring good cigars, preferably Cuban.

(In his confusion he reverts to touching the child on the head)

45

SMITH: What's wrong with him?

ANNAPURNA: Her.

SMITH: What's wrong with her?

ANNAPURNA: You call it pneumonia

SMITH: Hospital?

ANNAPURNA: She will only get it again.

SMITH: Can I help?

> *(She holds out her hand palm upwards for money. He gives her what he can immediately grab. But she keeps her hand out, looking at him blandly. He takes out wallet and gives her a note. She tucks it away)*

SMITH: Sure I can't help?

ANNAPURNA: pointing at his risen crutch) You look too busy helping yourself.

> *(To cover up, SMITH beckons for SINGH to come in and join him.*
>
> *They go into NANDI BABA's hut.*
>
> *In there, lighting shows the Baba now sitting on a very dilapidated Victorian armchair with a bottle of whiskey to his lips while he motions them to come inside.*
>
> *ANNAPURNA takes the opportunity of pushing past them to sit at the old man's feet.*
>
> *The BABA finishes swig, gurgles it, spits it out into the bottle, and then – with outrageous sudden viciousness -- rounds on SINGH)*

46

NANDI BABA: *I will kill you!*

(SINGH just sniggers awkwardly)

NANDI BABA: *Get out or dead meatski!*

(SINGH backs out but doesn't look too worried.

NANDI BABA reverts to cleaning his fingernails)

NANDI BABA: Honestly, some people go terribly impolite, don't you think?
   (and immediately)
Sit. Sit, sweet prince! Comezee all der vay in, if you're a...
   (screeches)
NOBODY!

SMITH: (shouting too) I SAID WHAT'D YOU DO WITH MY BOY!

(NANDI BABA smiles sweetly to him. He nudges ANNAPURNA to take the bottle of whiskey and to reach over to hand it to SMITH.

SMITH does take it but doesn't drink from it, just holds it)

NANDI BABA: So... I am a buggerlugs, nein?

SMITH: I'd say more a dopey bastard.

NANDI BABA: Then, my little cherry of a peach, comezee in und take a pew. Sorry, wrong church, you pathetic SOMEBODY. Anyvay, it is your fault more than your poor old lubberly priest ME. You barely gave me time to get on my smoking jacket und slippers while you were out dere trying to squeeze der root into my lady. Boy, some people, ja? Pardon me if my tits hangerzee down like real tits they are.

SMITH: Are you going to talk to me, or what?

47

NANDI BABA: Orf course. Off course, ha ha. Pardon my belly wumble. I do haf to dodge those pesky whale harpoons so, ja? Und now, sit sir, you poor misguided fool, since you were so fuchting rude to come in der eins-zwei-drei place.

> *(Suddenly NANDI BABA begins shouting a load of gibberish into the air, rolling his wild man's head from side to side and swinging his arms and legs so wildly that he smacks ANNAPURNA across the side of the head.*
>
> *She is felled and lies there... though still protecting the child... unmoving even after he calms down and uses her as a footstool.*
>
> *In the quietus – of SMITH's shock at all this – the old man speaks quietly and sensibly with no mock accent:)*

NANDI BABA: Ssh, you see. That blow to her konk was a mere swipe of history, a purely intention action and one that I am therefore above taking any responsibility for.

> *(He reaches across with his foot and prodded the back of her head with his toes. Still she doesn't move. He 'reverts' to histrionics)*

NANDI BABA: Sniff, sniff. Phew whiff. Stinky toes.

SMITH: You'd be no rose petal yourself.

NANDI BABA: Oh, no? Den you haf a nudder think commen, mein finklefunker.
     (then to the woman and to SMITH)
Now, get out, and you, buster, sit, you damn SOMEBODY of a fucking NOBODY!

> *(But SMITH remains standing defiantly, while ANNAPURNA gets up and leaves as told. She does it unhurriedly, brushes against SMITH and takes the whiskey bottle with her as she goes*

The NANDI BABA laughs, retrieves a grimy bottle of something yellow, tears out its cork with dangerous betel-stained teeth, and then waves what is surprising to Smith as being the genuine item:)

NANDI BABA: Sir, kindly partake of a shot of Martell Five-Star. Finished the first half off last night or last year. Never forget it. Get out of those ridiculous clothes. Go round with the old cods swinging in the scheme of things, ja and ha ha? Vait, Waitenzee oop. Before you have the cheek to take my good brandy, what do you want a cure for? Farting? Something to ward off some schiessenhaussen evil eye? Or for getting the undivided attention of your dirty-minded paramour with the shitty kid waiting out dere for you, you dirty rotten fokker of a scoundrel, you?

(Again suddenly, NANDI BABA cranks himself up with riveting energy, starts jumping up and down on the armchair as if winding up to a blind rage on a trampoline and begins ranting again:)

NANDI BABA: Vhich, vhich?, you fucking poor deluded simpleton?!

(He takes a full-bodied leap off the chair, passes Smith midair whirling his arms as if free-falling in space and is suddenly thundering out of the hut in full scream.

From her sitting position outside the door, ANNAPURNA looks in and motions to SMITH just to wait.

SINGH puts his head into the doorway)

SINGH: Mr Smith?

SMITH: Just give us a minute, Doctor.

(SINGH nods, withdraws.

49

SMITH waits. He only has to do so for a moment before NANDI BABA returns to stand in the doorway, in a parody of girlish coquettishness, with his fat forefinger tucked under his chin.

He giggles weirdly, then minces queanedly back to the armchair, settles himself back into a pose of sage contemplation)

NANDI BABA:
The self within me now is dead,
And thou enshrined in its stead.
Yea, this, I, Nandi, the Baba, testify,
No longer now is there "me" or "my".

SMITH: (growling) I was told you were serious in seeing me.

(NANDI BABA turns from coy to surly instantly. He grabs a square of old newspaper from a pile of newspapers cut neatly into squares and crashes down onto his backside to the earth floor.

There, motioning Smith to squat opposite, he starts drawing a yantra figure with an old ballpoint)

NANDI BABA: (all reasonableness) Und now, sweet prince, vwhere vwere vwe?

SMITH: You were trying to impress me with how loony-tunes you think you are.

NANDI BABA: Precisely. Gud for you. Is my table a banana crate or a crate for a Kraut? Now, you said you wanted something for your seedless balls?

SMITH: I want to hear about my boy Terry.

NANDI BABA: Ah, young Terrence.

SMITH: Yes.

NANDI BABA: I heard vat happened. I am sorry. Take a swig.

SMITH: I was told he hung around here. Why would that be?

NANDI BABA: That boy would have made a gud rat catcher, by gott!

SMITH: *What?*

NANDI BABA: You leave a baby alone und whammo the diddlio, he's gone with it. Vat thieving hands that munchin had!

> *(SMITH threatens to rise out of anger, but is, incomprehensively, shouted over:)*

NANDI BABA: SUMMA!
  (surprising coherent)
Summa! Don't take any notes; get Summa into your thick SOMEBODY head. Summa is the moment-to-moment of the Eternal Now. What fucking nonsense, but it is the first principle to remember which makes it the last thing you should be thinking about. Attain that and you have attained nothing; but you have to attain it because you must attain something, you frokkendisheit SOMEBODY. However, mein herr, it is not attainable so don't waste my time. All you haf is der Final Paradox which only idiots thinkenstein is final or even und paradox. So fuchting there, DOPEY!

SMITH: Who're you calling dopey?

> *(But NANDI BABA merely holds up his now-completed yantra squiggle, then stuffs it into his mouth and chews it with lip-smacking silliness.*
>
> *Then he spits this into a filthy, broken glass, and pushes it at SMITH:)*

NANDI BABA: Eat, drink und be frohlich. Slurp, slurp, you...
  (and actually spits thickly at Smith's feet)

... dummkopf klunkerhead SOMEBODY arsehole. Get NOBODY, gud und smart! Be deaf and blind to the opinions of others. Never be responsible for your actions, but you bloodyfuckingwell should be! All is opposite and all is paradox: attraction and repulsion, pleasure and pain, happiness and misery, heat and cold, life und death. Forget these, mein herr. They're bullshit. I'm sick of talking to you. IDIOT!'

(then suddenly sweetness and light:)
Drink, sweet prince.

SMITH: You have to be kidding.

NANDI BABA: DRINK!

SMITH: No fucking way.

NANDI BABA: Und gud thinking, if I may say so myself, mein herr.

(He is kneading the pulp on his thigh into a strand of fibre)

SMITH: What'd my Terry have to do with the rumour I've been told about this goddess roaring around here at night as half man, half cow?

NANDI BABA: Not cow, bull! Get it right, you dumbclucken chicken or piss off with your ignorance!

(Then he giggles again and leaps to his feet again, far quicker than Smith could follow. He is up on the armchair into his madman's jig again, this time giggling some nursery game)

NANDI BABA: In Twerry's cups. In his cups. In Twerry's cuppy wup wups...

SMITH: (shouting back just as crazy) BASTARD, WHAT'D YOU GET MY BOY INTO?!

(In shock, the BABA stops literally in midair. He stands there unsteadily on the armchair's cushion staring open-mouthed at Smith. He looks genuinely put down.)

NANDI BABA: Control yourself, mein herr! You are a guest in this house.

(He sits back pained, crosses his legs with esteemed modesty, and assumes the posture of a Hindu holy man in meditation. But his lips have gone all prissy. SMITH waits only so long...)

SMITH: You can go off like that for all you want, fatty, but I'll still be here waiting for an answer.

(NANDI BABA opens his eyes dreamily; they actually seem to be tearful)

NANDI BABA: I gave him nothing that a NOBODY of a SOMEBODY should not take if he or non-he wishing to see the Goddess as she really is or isn't, make up your mind. So there.
    (grins syrupy)
Perhaps mein herr should find out for himself?

SMITH: Name when and where!

NANDI BABA: (sweetly into air) When and where, was I asked?

SMITH: When and bloody where, blob butt!

NANDI BABA: (suddenly howling to the roof) OH, WELL! Aren't we a nosey old thing? Next full foolish moon, the pooja for ignoramuses like you, and there's visions to be had when they can't be had. You up to it, NOBODY?'

SMITH: You bet your fat arse!

NANDI BABA: Gut, mein herr. It will be an honour to have your company for the full Tantra ritual. Now GET OUT! But, hold, sweet prince, before you hurry off, tarry awhile, if you really feel you must.

(He reaches across and ties the now yantra 'string' around SMITH's wrist)

NANDI BABA: This'll perk up that pecker, you limp dick, so you can cuckold me with my woman, don't think I don't know your filthy mind.

    (and)

HELP, HELP, HELP, THAT'S ALL YOU GO ON ABOUT AND I'M SICK OF IT! The guard opens the dungeon door and asks the prisoner if he has any request since he's been there five years. Yes, a glass of water, the prisoner says. No problem. The guard opens the dungeon door after another five years and asks if the prisoner has any request after ten years now. Yes, the prisoner goes, a slice of bread would be nice. No worries. The guard opens the dungeon door after the next five years and asks any requests on his fifteen anniversary. Yes, a pillow for my head, goes the prisoner. Easy. De guard openszee the dungeon door after the next five years und asks if dere is any request for the prisoner's twentieth. No, thanks, says der prisoner. Thank Gott, says the guard; all you've done is bitch, bitch, bitch for the last twenty years.

    (back to all sweetness and light)

Incidentally, pecker-wise, keep this on for fifty-five days and partake of milk gruel as an offering to the Lord Shiva while reciting this mantra:

Om daridrano cinta-mani gunanika janmajabadho
Nimanganam dastram muraripu-varahasya bhavati

Don't bother to memorise it, just say it 1000 times a day for those fifty-five days. What does it say? It says pull the cotton wool out of your big fat ears, NOBODY. Of course, you could replace the milk gruel with Kellogg's cornflakes, up to you. Now get out, before I notice you are here and have you THROWN OUT!

SMITH (leaving) You expect me next full moon, fatso.

NANDI BABA: (childish mimic) 'You expect me next full moon, fatso.'

(back to charm)
Und don't forget to pick up a little baby takeaway on your way.

SMITH: What did you say?

NANDI BABA: Do not ignore der social graces, sweet prince.
Bring a baby.

SMITH: (half laugh) Where're I'm going to pick up a baby, you
nutter?

NANDI BABA: Oo, I don't know. Ask a nun for a takeaway. If
she won't give you one, give her a swift kick in the cunt.
Christian nuns would give anything to get a gud ole jackboot toe
in der crutch, yep sirree.

SMITH: You're joking or what?

NANDI BABA: Fuchtsake, man, don't start off comingzee empty
handed und being a social NOBODY, you NOBODY!

*(As sudden as any of his other surprised moves, NANDI
BABA leaps up and runs out of the hut screaming.*

*SMITH is used to this by now. He waits only a moment
before getting up and moving outside, where he sits down
on the ground with his back to the hut's wall, next to
ANNAPURNA.*

She already has her hand out for more money from SMITH.

*SMITH waves to SINGH that he is all right, while fishing in
his pocket for his wallet. He gives her some dollars. She
keeps her hand up... this is not begging or demanding just a
gesture... until he simply gives her all he's got.*

*While he does so, her child's hand creeps over and take a
gentle hold of his sleeve. Neither he nor her mother try to
remove it, but leave it attached to him)*

SMITH: (lovingly) Little thing.

ANNAPURNA: Yes.

SMITH: Doesn't she ever make any sound?

ANNAPURNA: Mostly not.

SMITH: But she's got a high fever most of the time?

(She nods, strokes the girl's head)

SMITH: You've got good English.
    (she nods)
Convent?
    (she nods)
That convent across the road there?
    (she nods)
How come? You here now, coincidence?

ANNAPURNA: (but dispassionately) I was raised there. I ran the office. It... ended.

SMITH: They say my son hung around there, here, a lot. Did you know him?

ANNAPURNA: I understood him.

SMITH: (pressing) But did you know him?

ANNAPURNA: I understood him.

(SMITH waits but there is obviously going to be no more)

SMITH: I take it that that priest of yours just ran away?

ANNAPURNA: (nodding) He saw you coming.

SMITH: Hey, I was just in there with him.

ANNAPURNA: (nodding again) Strange, isn't it?

SMITH: He saw me coming after I'd arrived and then ran off before I could get here? What if I go, is he going to see me stay?

(She shrugs with disinterest)

SMITH: And I suppose you believe this Hag Goddess...

ANNAPURNA: Chinnamasta.

SINGH: (echoing her from afar) Chinnamasta.

SMITH: Okay, okay. So you believe this charmer runs around at night eating unwanted babies and taking the sins of the father on Herself?

ANNAPURNA: Mother.

SMITH: Mother. Parents. The little'uns too. Phoofff! Shames all washed away?

(She waits as though waiting for him to ask a real question. She also gently removes her child's grip on his sleeve)

SMITH: (outcry) What did the old fool do with my boy?

ANNAPURNA: (quite openly) They took bhang.

SMITH: (dismissing that) Did he involve him in some village crap?

ANNAPURNA: (disarmingly) Of course.

SMITH: No, not 'of course'!

ANNAPURNA: (simply again) The yantras say you and I must go jiggy-jig.
     (pointing at his crutch)
Just look at yourself.

(SMITH looks down at his trousers, sees what she is seeing, quickly pulls his shirt out over his trousers to hide himself)

SMITH: God almighty.

SINGH: (calling out rebuke) Mr Smith, cover yourself!

SMITH: (back at him) I've got it.

SINGH: Hello?, I can see it from here.

SMITH: I said I've got it!

(SMITH gets to his feet, leaves ANNAPURNA. He is almost to SINGH when LINGAYYA emerges at the gate and blows his whistle at them. Imperiously, he beckons them to come to him)

SMITH: What's that prick doing here?

SINGH: (worried) I really don't know.

LINGAYYA: I ain't got all pissing day!

(SINGH, certainly, does as commanded and hurries towards the Superintendent. SMITH follows at his leisure.

Blackout)

8.

(READER SMITH fills in the interim:)

READER SMITH: 'This's where it'll start getting all fuzzy, Helen. You were the writer. You would've made better heads and tails of it. You should've come instead of sending me.
    (pause)

58

So, yes, that dog of a creature Lingayya turns up there. He clicks his obnoxious fingers and we go trotting after his tap-tap-tap like puppies. You see, behind the Nandi Baba's were those shitty mangrove swamps bleeding into the canal. Around that Manvoor town, make that great rubbish tip not mangrove swamp.'

(and)

'That old coot mentioned jackboots. Well, bastard Lingayya only wore old sandals but he could have been wearing jackboots. He didn't look back; he just strode us in and out these squelching paths to some sort of cess pool, where he just stood with that smirk of his pointing at this filthy pond or pool or bog or some damn thing. I mean, it was disgusting. It had these slippery mud-slide sides down to a stinking patch of water like thick soup and stunk to high hell. A great heap of shit floating down the canal over time had clogged it up like this was *it* for rubbish... filth heaven. Methane gas... something more... If it hadn't been for Lingayya being there I could well have heaved up.'

(Lighting up on SMITH, SINGH and LINGAYYA at the edge of a steaming bog)

READER SMITH: 'The thing was, as I say, he was pointing that shitting lathi of his at this spew-making pool... honestly, liquid kakk... and just standing there all chest-puffed-out. I started to see ripples, like something was moving under there... something monstrous. I pointed. I managed...'

SMITH: What's that?

LINGAYYA: What do you think, *puta*?

(At the same time, a mud-caked head dramatically emerges from the grime, then NANDI BABA's leering face, then his gross naked torso.

He lifts his arms from out of the pool having to strain against the sucking hold the oozing liquid has on them.

59

He holds up a rotting corpse of a baby in each hand. He cackles as though this is the greatest joke in the world. He holds them up in outstretched arms as they drip grume.

Then he slowly sinks back into the shocking fetid water with the bodies.

A long pause, which LINGAYYA is obviously enjoying.

LINGAYYA turns away and goes to move off.

SINGH calls quickly after him)

SINGH: Inspector, give us a lift!

LINGAYYA: I'm following not carrying.
   (points to SMITH)
Let that bugger sweat.

(He leaves.

SMITH and SINGH are too shocked to move immediately.

SMITH realises NANDI BABA hasn't resurfaced)

SMITH: Where's the Baba?!

SINGH: (shrugging) By now he'll be floating down the canal.

SMITH: Oh, God.

SINGH: No, no, hello? Washing the mud off or maybe the fat off the mud.

(Blackout)

(end Act 1)

Act 2
9.

(Lighting up on the SINGH's dining room, where SMITH and SINGH are sitting at meal places while LAKSHMI fusses around setting and constantly adjusting the table setting. It is lunch.

It is very noticeable that there are two places extra set.

READER SMITH plays his light around and momentarily settles on the Kali-Chinnamasta stature. He doesn't linger on it very long.)

READER SMITH: 'The next day, Smith felt manic, full of energy. He couldn't sleep; he had things to do, manic energy to spread around under a lot of lazy arses. But it was some sort of holiday, some day before Pooja night. He went to church, the Christian one there, the Catholic Christian one, but this was no place for his manic energy, so he sat there hating the long-haired middle-aged beached hippy of a priest. He didn't know why. Only mania can see around corners. Then he went through those streets like a dose of salts, not at all fazed by being just another manic atom out for one of their random collisions. He manically came across a communications bureau. He manically went in and manically tried to ring you and then manically decided against it and manically ran out. He had, yes, until lunch. Then after lunch he manically had his appointment at that effer Lingayya's place but didn't know beforehand he would also manically crash back into that church and manically raid the priest's manse. All was being set in manic motion...

(pause)

except, thank God, his crutch. Without that woman Annapurna anywhere in sight, that stayed behaving itself, the maniac of a thing. Still, this showing now was before any of that happened...'

(Fade for the play area – with SMITH, LAKSHMI and SINGH -- to become dominant and:)

LAKSHMI: (fussing around them) Germaine. Kaput.

SINGH: Hello, hello, my dear? German not germaine. And he's only half so. And Kapalika not kaput.
    (to SMITH)
It's her word's day. She likes picking up on English sounds on her word day. It's the day most guests like to take tours very early when she has just got up and tuned her ears.

LAKSHMI: It is what has made India more greatly known, Mr Smith. We all have our bit to play, hai? Are you all right? Your eyes are going round and round your head.

SINGH: (rebuking) Hello, my dear.

SMITH: No, it's all right. A bit agitated, that's all.

LAKSHMI: Exactly! You believe who you want to, Mr Smith. All an Indian lady can say to you is the Nandi Baba is Germaine by way of Kapalika, hint-hint. Don't you worry, Mr Smith; you just listen to these lips only. That silly old Nandi Baba is a kaput of the first order you won't find in any guide book in this establishment.

SINGH: Mrs Singh means, Mr Smith, a Tantric priest who follows the extreme Hindu sect, the Kapalikas. They are our country's holy terrors.

SMITH: You mentioned it. Yeah, but this old fruitcake...

LAKSHMI: Fruitcake?

SINGH: It's a fruitcakey term for a fruitcake, Mrs Singh.

LAKSHMI: Usable?

SINGH: Given today being today, by all means, log it in, my dear.

(They wait politely for SMITH to continue)
62

SMITH: I was just saying Nandi Baba... he's not wandering the streets raving around. He's on his fat quoit swilling good brandy, and not-so-politely farting. Excuse me, Mrs S. And if he's not seeping top-drawer Amani out from under the armpits, I don't know what.
  (to SINGH's look)
And I'm never going to forget the old fool rising out of that bog hole holding those two...

  (He is cautioned by SINGH about his wife being within earshot. Of course LAKSHMI sees this but merely politely leaves to come in and out bringing in the food, while:)

SINGH: Because of whatever we were talking about, the Kapalikas have to go around begging food with a human skull like their Lord. But, yes, hello?, Nandi Baba has graduated past all that. All that he has left is a skull on his palm.

SMITH: Yes, I've seen that on... somebody's palm.

LAKSHMI: Aha, that woman!
  (delighted at SMITH's reaction)
Look at the poor man blush! What a show he gave outside the hut, I hear! Bravo, Mr Smith!

SINGH: (covering up) Hello?, Mr Smith, you see the Kapalika's Lord Bhairava was also denied worldly pleasures while having to sport...
  (calls out to her)
another word that might qualify, my dear.

LAKSHMI: (nearby repeat) Sport.

SINGH: (back to SMITH) ...sport a perpetual priapism the Lord Bhairava could never use.

LAKSHMI: (on her way in) Since then we Indians are always trying, Mr Smith. You just look at our terrific world-record Guinness-Book-of-Records population.

(then to her husband)
You show Mr Smith yours, Dr Singh.

SINGH: Hello?

LAKSHMI: ('only fair') Mr Smith has been showing you his.

SINGH: (shocked) Hello?, how do you know that, Mrs Singh?

LAKSHMI: ('Hollywood') You can smell it a mile off, baby.

SINGH: (over her) Nandi Baba has graduated from wandering. The Lord Bhairava finally had his sins washed away in the sacred river, don't you know, Mr Smith. So like Nandi Baba, their priests can get penance too by doing some very big service.

SMITH: He forks out free erections?

SINGH: (strangely guarded) Community service, hello?

SMITH: Free erections, community service?

SINGH: No, no, hello? Other things.

SMITH: What sort of community service could that old whacko ever do?

SINGH: I think my wife might be best qualified to explain that.

(She affects modesty in taking up the offer of being centre-stage)

LAKSHMI: First let me say, you would have been interested to see his, Mr Smith.

SMITH: (doubtfully) Absolutely.

LAKSHMI: As to that other matter... and I have heard only what these ears let in, mind... the Baba helps those backwards people over evil-there with teeny baby problems.

64

SMITH: Teeny problems?

LAKSHMI: (nodding) No more teenier. You heard that from the low-down, Mr Smith, not from me.

SMITH: You should have seen what that old dingdong pulled out of that shithole... sorry, sorry.

LAKSHMI: I did, Mr Smith. And it was terribly yuk-drippy, don't you think?

SINGH: Hello?, what do you mean you did, my dear?

LAKSHMI: ('Hollywood' again) I ain't no stoolie rat, honey.

SINGH: You were there, hello?

> *(She knows a good suspense situation when she sees one, goes out, returns with two more plates of food which she carefully lays at the two empty set places. Finally deigns to explain:)*

LAKSHMI: I didn't see what the Baba was holding up,
    (again, movie talk)
but I can sure guess, brother.
    (to her husband's amazed look)
Well, the police boat was a bit too far offshore, Doctor.

SINGH: The police boat.

LAKSHMI: ('simple') Inspector Lingayya said he was going to follow you and I booked a place by plonking the old scratch-mine-I'll-scratch-yours down in his boat. Tax-payers' money.
    (adds when theatrically ripe)
Well, it would have something to do with the teeny baby problems over in that evils place and I have personally heard I am more in favour of sinking them in there than letting them float off and end up out at sea blocking up the international shipping lanes. What would passing seafarers think of us Indians, Doctor?

SMITH: (incredulous) You're talking foetus... things?

LAKSHMI: Of course, kiddo!

SINGH: Hello, hello, not 'of course', my dear!

LAKSHMI: Well, if there's other things, they haven't reached these ears, Doctor.
    (then to SMITH)
Anyway, you get the drift, don't you, kiddo?

SMITH: (dully) The drift.

SINGH: Remember the word-sound day, Mr Smith!

(She waves her husband off)

LAKSHMI: Well, you have given us food for thought, like any good Aussie traveller, Mr Smith. We have not thought to put free male upstandings in our brochures for all to see, but will consider it. On our side of the ferry, it is a lot easier than over there. All we ladies over here have to do is snap our fingers.

SINGH: (no little outrage) Hello, hello?

LAKSHMI: My husband is one of the best, you know.

SINGH: Hello?

LAKSHMI: Nor should you worry about it, Mr Smith. I have been a guide in my time and I can assure you, where there a bit of mud in India, you find all sorts of interesting things popping up.

(To cover up, SMITH indicates the two vacant places she had blithely fully served:)

SMITH: Expecting more guests?

SINGH: (relieved to change subject) Our son and daughter-in-law, Mr Smith. They are away in Mumbai.

(LAKSHMI puts chutneys etc on their plates)

SMITH: Really missing them, are you?

LAKSHMI: Oh no, Mr Smith! They can't be missing if they are eating hearty here, hai?

SMITH: Sorry, I didn't mean missing like that.

SINGH: Hello? We always set places for our son and his wife when they're away, Smithee. If they know they are eating well at home, they won't ever have to wonder where their next meal is coming from when they're away. Superstitious nonsense, I suppose.

SMITH: Not at all, I suppose.

SINGH: We don't like to suppose when it comes to our children.

SMITH: I suppose not.

LAKSHMI: You poor man, eat more. I can see your bones from here. This is not a good advertisement for our kitchen. Also you should hurry towards my dessert, Mr Smith.
    (pulls a bit of paper from her apron)
I will read what out last Sweden lady left lying under her bed...
    (reads)
'I discovered her ras gula dessert was matured cheese balls soaked in a bowl of fast-congealing ghee mixed with globules of raw molasses. I discovered the ingredients in a real hurry in the middle of the night. I had to lick my lips a lot while on my knees bending over the bowl...' That is what is coming your way, Mr Smith.

SMITH: It's just that I don't want to be late for Lingayya's.

LAKSHMI: That man can wait.

SINGH: No, he can't, my dear!

LAKSHMI: I kept him waiting while I got into his boat yesterday.

SINGH: I bet you did, my dear.

LAKSHMI: You betcha bottom booties, kiddo!

(Blackout.

10.

(In the interim:)

READER SMITH: 'No one was what anyone seemed to be, was right, Helen. Dr Singh told me Lingayya's place was one of the grandest in the town. He had to be right there. It was a mansion as garish as Lingayya himself was jet-black sinister. From outside, three floors of grey-and-shocking-pink tiles made it look like an attack of leprosy. Its fourth floor was rendered in cry-out purple with yellow window frames. Its ten-foot-high boundary wall was quartered out in black and brown. A butler-type of guy who looked older than Gandhi would be now was waiting for them at the rose-varnish front door. When he nodded follow-me his neck cracked. It did. The place had the musty smell of old books, an old library, paper pulp, old inks of magazines and newspapers, instead of like a cave of a gorilla like Smith expected.
     (then)
His impression of a library wasn't wrong. Lingayya was on the third floor, up the top of a library ladder, a ledger in one hand and somehow tending tomes on shelves that were floor-to-ceiling, walnut and rosewood, exquisitely rendered, crammed with volumes. There was even a grandfather clock that chimed four o'clock with deep sleepiness. No, not a library; more like a treasury. Smith felt like every room in the place would be the same.

(and)

Would you believe, bloody Lingayya had what looked like a smoking jacket on over his sarong. There was nothing of the police thuggee tap-tapping about him. Rather, he was the doyen of the richest family in the district then, who delved out fishing licenses on his ships and boats, and delving out raw justice wasn't in it. The unpleasant dork only nodded slightly at their entrance, though, and he didn't deign at first to get down from what he undoubtedly felt was his proper greater height.

(Lighting comes up on LINGAYYA, SMITH and SINGH)

LINGAYYA: I hear you are a lover of books too, Smith, maybe not just a *picker* like a crow. If it would help, you are welcome to escape into my humble library at any time. Phone ahead when nobody's home to answer it.

> *(SINGH sees warning signs in the open animosity between the other two, and keeps trying to ameliorate it:)*

SINGH: Good afternoon, Inspector.

> *(He gets a nod without LINGAYYA's eyes leaving SMITH)*

LINGAYYA: Right, it's my day off and my humble abode, so I'm doing the talking.

SMITH: Or what? Out comes the bamboo tickle stick?

> *(LINGAYYA merely parries this as not warranting any attention. He goes back to finish what he has been writing in his ledger)*

LINGAYYA: Right you are.

SMITH: Yoo hoo, we're down here, mate.

LINGAYYA: Sure you are. Where else would a mate like you be? Certain passers-by of the book shelves of life may not be aware but we Lingayyas have here just over three hundred thousand volumes of rare and priceless books which would probably give a 'mate' a headache. There are ten thousand nineteenth-century first editions in Tamil... a language that doesn't get choked by more than twenty-six letters of the alphabet... and about the same in Malayalam and Hindi. There are some five thousand first-edition books on our medicines, one hundred and fifty thousand Indian traditional poetries in all language except that slug-under-a-rock Shakespeare. There are religious books and tracts and manuscripts, two hundred thousand books of regional-language short stories, two thousand articles on the deities and the Prophet by Indian authors, about a half a dozen on your Jesus Christ, lucky to get a look-in. I have finally said no to the Congress Library of America pestering us to our thousands of volumes on Islam's nature that were banned in the days of the Partition.

    (snort down to SMITH)

Over what would they want to buy off your family, *mate*?

SMITH: Not my assessment of yours, for sure.

SINGH: Hello?

LINGAYYA: My family could be said to have been the librarians to the Independence movement in this country. Yours?

SMITH: We sing the national anthem on Australia Day and that's rich and rare.

LINGAYYA: Yes, I bet. You see around you, Smith, the largest and rarest private collections in India and possibly Asia. And I have what I believed to be an exceedingly genuine second edition of Donatus's Latin school grammar printed at Mainz by either Gutenberg or Fust in 1460. That misprint of the date makes it a rare item to sing about on your Australia Day. Notwithstanding that, we Lingayyas came here by camel, by tent, by the Malabar sea routes, by buffalo carts. Nobody came in and tried to pick away at us. That, we never allowed. You see our books here? All of them have been read from cover to cover, from what-for to

what-for. There is not one shelved here that we've allowed to be *picked* at.
    (then with real menace)
We do in anyone, any shithead from anywhere, who tries to come in and pick at us Lingayyas.

SMITH: Good for you.

LINGAYYA: (sudden good cheer) Well, look at that. Prayer time.

> *(He climbs down from his library ladder, goes over to sit on a floor mat with cushion.*
>
> *SMITH and SINGH wait for him to begin whatever prayers he is talking about. But they are left stranded, because LINGAYYA does not do any prayers)*

LINGAYYA: (gruffly) Are we going to be all day?

SMITH: Prayers?

LINGAYYA: I said it was prayer time. I did not say I was going to do prayers.
    (to SINGH)
See, Doctor, there's that *pick-pick* his type can't help. Can you get him to sit instead of *nit picking* at us?

> *(SMITH and SINGH take their places on the mat opposite LINGAYYA)*

SMITH: You wanted to see me?

LINGAYYA: Your son...

SMITH: No, first of all, tell us what that was yesterday at that stink hole with the fat priest?

71

LINGAYYA: Sure. To stop you starting to pick at something else. Nandi Baba does a community service you don't trouble yourself with, Smith.

SMITH: Those were two little baby things!

LINGAYYA: Very observant of you.

SMITH: You're the law around here and you showing me that? For all I know, that wasn't some pretend stuff. Those little things come from being chucked in there, and don't bullshit me otherwise.

LINGAYYA: So? Your point?

SMITH: So there could be more of the little things down in that ooze for all I know.

SINGH: Hello...?

LINGAYYA: (brushing off mediation) There could. Oh, there could. You want to go *picking* around in that?
    (gets very menacing to SMITH)
Just shut up. I said it's my place and I'm doing the talking.
    (waits, gets silence)
Old Nandi Baba is doing our people over there a service that you couldn't possibly begin to understand, *mate*. He takes many of the unfortunate little ones from the Catholic nuns' hands. How does that happen? If you must know, many of the babies left outside there are dead... yes, yes, maybe even killed...

SMITH: Little shes.

LINGAYYA: So what?

SMITH: Not little hes.

LINGAYYA: And? I said I was doing the talking! The nuns take them in. No baptizing, no way. But they at least record the little things who it's too late baptising for, even give them names, and then return their bodies at least to the community they came from, as they should. They do that through Nandi Baba. He is the priest who says yes I'll take them, who else? Down there, where you were, in that, sure, shit hole, its parents or parent can come along in the dead of night and have their bad feelings about abandoning the child washed away by the Baba. And any baby sins that came with it too. That's how it's done. That's how it should be done, *mate*.

(he turns to SINGH)
You're the Coroner. You tell him.

SINGH: Unmarked graves are all the same, no, Mr Smith? And the Nandi Baba, hello?, invokes the Goddess to absolve their sins through him. That's how I understand it. It violates no regulation, don't you know.

SMITH: The Goddess being that Hag charmer we saw the statue of?

LINGAYYA: You don't call Her Hag, Smith. You don't bring your foreign smirks here.

SMITH: Don't bring your local smirks here! Jesus, my Terry was found among your boats.

LINGAYYA: So? Your point?

SMITH: You've already said that.

LINGAYYA: True. Yes, he was. A couple of the lads must have thought him up to no good. It was dark... and you know yourself how dangerous it is to go around *picking* at things.

SMITH: Is that a threat?

SINGH: Of course it wasn't, hello?

LINGAYYA: Of course it was.

73

SMITH: Terry wasn't around the boats. He was around the convent all the time. And why was that?

LINGAYYA: Who knows why? Who cares? All I know is like-father-like-son, he was poking his nose in between the work of the nuns and Nandi Baba when there's nothing there for him to be pick-picking over. That's the *picking* I can't abide.
(then)
Don't you try it. Leave it alone. It's all wrapped up.

SMITH: And you don't like *picking*.

LINGAYYA: That's right, foreigner. You've been warned.

SMITH: I guess you could say I have been.

SINGH: Hello, Mr Smith? It's good to have the Inspector give us his time.

SMITH: (chastened) Yeah... okay.

LINGAYYA: Now I'm going to tell you why I told the Doctor here to bring you here to see me when I heard you were coming to visit us.
(then fires in)
Are you so thick-headed you didn't think your son would find out about his twin sister they didn't give you at that adoption agency?

(SMITH is taken aback)

SMITH: Louise?

LINGAYYA: Call her what you will. Smita, they named her. They took her off the Mumbai streets around the age of seven and brought her back here to the convent. The nuns raised her. She became one of them... Sister Smita in fact.

SMITH: How?

74

LINGAYYA: (enjoying his discomfort) How what, naming her Smita?

SMITH: How did Terry find out.

LINGAYYA: Schee, man, he only had to ask. You only had to ask. The stink you made at the time's all over our records. Maybe you kept *picking* away at your own son too and that's why he obviously didn't tell you. Bad luck, *puta*.
   (and)
Dr Singh, you tell him the Coroner bit.

SINGH: (carefully, sadly) Mr Smith, your Terry never met her. He couldn't, you see. Five, six, years ago, Sister Smita was found at the bottom of the convent's well. We tried but, apart from rumours, we didn't find any foul play. It was before dawn one night.

LINGAYYA: (still enjoying it) Rumours.

SINGH: (shaking head) I'm just the Coroner.

LINGAYYA: (taking it up, enjoying it) Rumours someone did her away after 'she'd witnessed some shameful act', as the CID report said. It got to be your Catholic Church's dirty business, who cares? All we know is what her nun friends told Terry.

SMITH: How do you know what they told him?

LINGAYYA: (leer) We convinced him he should tell us. That woman Annapurna you look so keen on, she won't talk about how she got that girl. Five years old. Funny that. And that long-haired Christian priest they won't promote or move from here, he won't look out from under his migraines.

SINGH: ('the doctor') They are quite severe, don't you know, Inspector.

LINGAYYA: Up his Christian nit-picker, too.
   (rounds on SMITH again)

So you go around and ask a few questions from them, instead of *picking* at the wrong people, foreigner.

(LINGAYYA suddenly rises, leaves them without standing on ceremony. As he goes:)

LINGAYYA: Now, call the butler yourselves. He knows the way to the front door. Don't pick its lock, mate.

(Blackout)

11.

(Outside the Singh's boarding house.

As lighting comes up:)

READER SMITH: 'Yes, our little Louise. Smita. Sister Smita. "Done away with by someone because she'd witnessed a shameful act", or however it went. Ah, Helen, Helen. That poor little she we didn't even get to set eyes on, and we couldn't do a thing to...
    (has to stop)
We should've made her so happy. We wanted to make her so happy, remember? How they came into that damn adoption waiting room without her. I know it will still break your heart. Now you know why I can only write this to you. Our Louise. They threw her back like soiled goods.
    (then)
Would've we have been good for her?... I mean, did we make our Terry happy? Was it a good life after all? So you tell me... why didn't he phone or message that he'd learnt about having a twin sister? Was he disgusted with us, that we were somehow to blame for everything that happened to the poor little thing? Please don't let me think that. I don't want to think that...'

(He fades for 'play level'.

SMITH shows surprise he has come by ANNAPURNA and her child sitting outside the boarding house under the fertility clinic's sign:)

SMITH: (to SINGH) You go on.

(SINGH nods goes inside. SMITH stands 'over' ANNAPURNA since they are in the middle of one of the town's main street and:)

SMITH: What does the old goat want now?

ANNAPURNA: Old goat, no.

SMITH: I've got a bone to pick with him, too. Tell him I'm coming to nail his doo-doo before the full moon.

ANNAPURNA: He is not at home.

SMITH: He ran away again? He fooling me around still?

ANNAPURNA: He ran when he heard you know your son was finding out something about Sister Smita.

SMITH: How could the old drip know that?'

ANNAPURNA: (obviously) He saw it.

SMITH: Here we go again.

ANNAPURNA: He saw it.

SMITH: Okay, I'll bite again. How did he see it?

(She merely points to the centre of her forehead)

SMITH: 'Kay. So he ran where?'

ANNAPURNA: (equally obvious) Out the back door when he saw you coming.

(frankly pointing to his crutch)
He is still right.

> *(SMITH is now again crouched so that passers-by don't notice his state)*

SMITH: (effort to divert her eyes) I'm up here.

ANNAPURNA: (very amused) Are you?

> *(Now he finds it best to kneel in front of her to communicate:)*

SMITH: How's the girl?

> *(ANNAPURNA shrugs, brings her cheek down to the child's head)*

ANNAPURNA: She will be all right soon.

SMITH: Don't you give her anything? Pain killers?

> *(The woman merely looks at him; it is enough of an answer)*

SMITH: Look, I wanted to ask you something tomorrow. I'll ask it now...?

> *(She nods permission. He points to the little girl)*

SMITH: How old? Five or six?
   (she doesn't need to answer)
Look... you were working in the convent's office... managing it... didn't you say?

ANNAPURNA: Yes.

SMITH: What happened that you left? Was it because of your child... like being big with sort of?

ANNAPURNA: Me and the priest?

SMITH: Well, yes, maybe.

ANNAPURNA: No.

SMITH: (appalled at not knowing) God, I don't even know her name.

ANNAPURNA: She has no name.

SMITH: Why not?

ANNAPURNA: (shrugging) She was not mine then. She is now. She was one of Nandi Baba's nobodies.

(He thinks to laugh, but she doesn't)

SMITH: Are you serious?

ANNAPURNA: She was handed over to him by the nuns, but he found she was alive.

(She just stares at him, will give no more information)

SMITH: Did you know Sister Smita?
   (gets small wary nod)
I did and didn't. We called her little Louise. Once upon a time.

ANNAPURNA: She was my friend. We grew up together.

SMITH: In the convent or the streets?

ANNAPURNA: Both.

SMITH: I'm sorry.
   (then 'plunges in')
What happened to her... did she see something that made you leave the convent?

*(ANNAPURNA waves her free hand in the air as though
warding off wrong things. She rises and moves off)*

SMITH: (after her) I'm going to see that priest!

(She stops, looks back at him)

SMITH: I'm not talking of Nandi Baba.

ANNAPURNA: (knowing that) He has migraines.

SMITH: I'll give him migraines!

(But she has moved off.

*Just as he can begin to straighten up, she returns, having
forgotten:)*

ANNAPURNA: I was sent to say your Tantra will not be inside
but outside.

SMITH: Where?

ANNAPURNA: (shrugs) Outside. By the fire.

(She leaves now.

He calls after her)

SMITH: By 'the fire', you mean the old dope's mud swimming
pool?

(He gets no reply.

Blackout)

12.

*(Inside the SINGH's boarding house, around the dining
table, with LAKSHMI bustling around setting up tea)*

LAKSHMI: Mr Smith, Mr Smith.

SMITH: Mrs Singh, Mrs Singh.

LAKSHMI: Call me Lakshmi or I'll call you bee's knees.

SINGH: Hello, hello?

LAKSHMI: Drink your tea, Doctor.

SINGH: It's too hot, Mrs Singh.

LAKSHMI: Blow hard like a die-hard Bruce Willis, Dr Singh.
    (turns to SMITH)
You do your die-hard Bruce Willis best, too, Mr Smith.

SMITH: I'm really trying.

LAKSHMI: I saw you outside with that woman and child, Mr
Smith. As a tourist who has to pace himself in our excitable
region, you should be careful where your blood flows in your
foreign body. I saw some of our schoolchildren with the excellent
grades pointing and giggling.

SINGH: Hello?, that's none of our business, my dear.

SMITH: Yes, it is, if you don't mind. I think I'm going to need
more help.

LAKSHMI: We are all ears, dear sir.

SMITH: Well... look... if you don't mind me asking...

LAKSHMI: 'If I'm going to take my son Terry home...', is that
what you are going to say?

SMITH: (nodding, to SINGH) If I'm going to take my boy home, don't I need some sort of autopsy or Coroner report from you first?

LAKSHMI: (rounds on SINGH too) Yes, where is that dangblasted thing?

>*(This is more like it for SINGH. He settles back into an official stance:)*

SINGH: Hello, hello? As to that, we don't mind you asking in the least you see. A little delay in the lab, apparently. The laboratory technician, Mr Smith, is going on strike over your Terry's tissues and the resultant unpaid overtime.

SMITH: Come again?

SINGH: I know what you mean. She is saying overseas tissue take a whole lot longer than local tissue. I said to her, don't get silly; tissue is tissue. She said how does she know foreign tissue is the same until she finds out whether it is overseas tissue. We could send away, of course, but... I don't suppose you could help us out with a little slice or two, could you?

SMITH: No!
    (then)
Jesus, if it helps.

LAKSHMI: (rolling it around her tongue) 'Jesus, if it helps'.

SINGH: (rebuke) Hello, hello, my dear?
    (back to SMITH)
Thank you. We shall keep that in mind. But first, a little bit of another snag is that, though she is quite good at chess, don't you know, she is a bit inexperienced when it comes to tissue and meat.

SMITH: Meat.

LAKSHMI: (repeat) Meat.

SINGH: Meat. Precisely.

(and stops)

SMITH: Meat?

SINGH: Well, you take a good old heart or liver and chop off a chunk of meat. That's easy. You know where you stand with a chunk of heart or liver. Cut and go, as it were. But tissues are finicky. They can play havoc with the technical staff's tea breaks and overtimes, don't you know. Tissues curl up into troublesome slithers, especially, apparently, when you don't know where they've come from. And your Terry is also so much tissue, hai?
    (in the stunned silence)
And it'll look very bad if she strikes over meat, rather than tissue, you see.

SMITH: (sudden outcry) There is nothing is this to get my boy killed!

LAKSHMI: Look what you have done, Dr Singh! Shame!

SINGH: Hello?, what did I do?

LAKSHMI: If you don't know, sir, how am I to know? What am I going to tell the next guest who walks through that door?

SINGH: (miserably) I don't know! Tell them we're working on it!

LAKSHMI: And what is 'it', do tell these waiting lug'oles of mine.

SINGH: *I don't know!*

SMITH: I'll need that report if you say I need it.

SINGH: And you'll get it, Mr Smith.

LAKSHMI: Okeydokey, that's settled, then.

(She fills cups again. When it comes to the two extra places, she removes the full tea cups, replaces them with new ones and fills those)

SMITH: I see your son and daughter-in-law aren't back yet.

LAKSHMI: My son's such a stickler for his tea, Mr Smith.

SMITH: No tea in Mumbai?

LAKSHMI: ('Hollywood') Ha, he wouldn't touch their muck with a barge pole, dude.

(Having served all the tea necessary, she stops and looks more closely at SMITH. Seeing pain, she quite frankly turns him around from the table and positions him between her legs. She pats him sympathetically over the ears with both hands at once, then cradles his torso against her ample belly. Her breasts rest perfectly on the top of his head)

SINGH: (a bit appalled) Hello, hello?

LAKSHMI: (crooning) Ssh, Mr Smith. Silence is the good oil for bumps and bruises. Poor you. Poor little baby girl lost to you by those people. Poor little Sister Smita. I have heard what happened from the good doctor here. Poor boy Terry of yours. More of your sorry history comes to these ears before you as each day goes by. What a mess and having to cope with all those erections! What a funny little tourist you are! Please, Mr Smith, I cannot have you feeling the two-into-one blues. We are trying to make it a reportable offence to the bed-and-breakfast board of India. Would I lie, honey pie?

SMITH: (coming up for air) One eye would never cheat the other, Mrs Singh.

LAKSHMI: (delighted) You betcha little baby booties.

(She can now release SMITH with all due conscience, and:)

LAKSHMI: Now, do you need a cut lunch for going to hit on that long-haired Father Michael of the Catholic persuasion?

SMITH: You heard about him, too.

LAKSHMI: I did not hear it first, but I can assure you it hasn't gone out the other ear.
     (goes 'Hollywood' yet again)
You sink it into the sucker, kiddo!

SINGH: Hello, hello?

LAKSHMI: (lips pursed) Dr Singh, everybody within the big shout knows what happened between that man and that woman with the child and that poor little nun who should have been Mr Smith's.

   (Her certainty brings SMITH up short)

SMITH: Tell me!

LAKSHMI: And as soon as I find out, I will, Mr Smith, you put your last dime on it, dollface.

   (SMITH is really let down)

SINGH: Hello, my dear, see what you have done?

LAKSHMI: (gangster mouth) My man Smith will tear the bum to pieces.

SINGH: Hello, hello...?

LAKSHMI: (ignoring him) If you don't take a cut lunch, remember there's a Chinese take-away just across the street, Mr Smith.

SINGH: My wife means the church is only on the next block, doesn't she, Mrs Singh?

LAKSHMI: He needs more meat on his bones, Dr Singh, that's what I mean.

(She proudly claps SMITH on the back to 'go, go', and he does go with real driven energy.

Blackout)

13.

(Lighting up on READER SMITH)

READER SMITH: 'That ceiling fan. Those ceiling fans. Their things that go around wheel-wheeling, urn-turning...
(and)
Lakshmi Singh had revived Smith, Helen. Suddenly, he felt manic again, full of that rare, different type of energy there. He leapt out of the room, ran down the corridor, opened the front door manically and leapt manically out into the street. Make way for the mighty Woods! Australia thundering through!...'

(Blackout)

14.

(SMITH returns to the boarding house from the church, where the SINGHs are waiting.

He is desolate, yet still angry. He shrugs his shoulders to indicate very little was accomplished.

As the lighting comes back up on READER SMITH, up on the play area (and even though it looks she is mime-acting

86

*out what SMITH is relating), LAKSHMI enacts what
SMITH is obviously relating about his attempt to see the
Catholic priest Father Michael. She is all silent-movie
dramatic, does quite a good job at following:)*

READER SMITH: Helen, nothing. Da nada. You had to see that
Father Michael to believe him. He was right out of the Flower
Generation... like stuck in it... a 70s Lover Boy, with Lord
Fauntleroy locks and a floral bandanna around his head. Even his
vestment had to have been nipped'n'tucked in at the waist. What
a ponce!

*(behind him, LAKSHMI acts the Father mincing around,
&ce:)*

READER SMITH: 'Smith got there for evening mass. Five
people were in the whole place.
    (LAKSHMI searches the far horizon)
Mighty popular Father Michael was, right? So Smith waited as
long as he could while he's going on with the Mass until his manic
energy got the best of him and he stood up in the middle of the
church and shouted, 'Your priest's a load of crud', or something
like that, to which the Father stopped in midstream with this shock
on his face, especially when someone else yelled out, 'Ain't that
the truth', or something. And then Smith shouted, 'What did you
do to the Annapurna woman and my little girl Louise, you
bugger?'
    (LAKSHMI reels back)
And then that Michael Fr., would you believe, Helen, he reeled
back under a migraine attack, held both hands to his temples, then
simply turned and took off. He did. He bolted from the altar in
communion midstream.
    (LAKSHMI runs around with her arms waving panic)
Smith shouldn't have done it like that. But he had. Pretty soon he
was the only one waiting for the Mass to begin again. He waited
twenty minutes and then gave up. He went around the back to the
Manse. Still nobody. He heard plates and thought bugger-it. He
followed the sound down corridors and curtains and into the
priests' kitchen. And there the little poncey sod was...'

(LAKSHMI sits at the table, rests on her arms in an encompassing gesture of 'all this food's mine' and follows the action:)

READER SMITH: 'at table, as they say. I kid you not. He had laid out in front of him dishes Smith presumed were multiple curries and fruits, and, despite looking taut, trim and cholesterol-terrific -- rather than migraine-struck as Smith had been told -- he was obviously relishing the fact that all of it was all eminently mittable, and only his. He was leaning forward, his arms circling all the dishes he could, his hands formed into clutching claws as though he was about to scoop up the plates and give them all one big hug. His shoulder-length black hair bobbed coquettishly as he chuckled over what looked like a large bowl of soup like some fat abbot alone at last in the creamery. When he looked up and saw Smith, it went something like this:

'Nup', went Smith, 'Not good enough, flower! What'd they let you get away with?'

'*Who*?', he went.

'I'll give you 'shameful act', you little bugger,' Smith went.

Then Michael FJ Ringlets lets out this pathetic, corny 'Ow!', gripped his forehead against a pantomime of another migraine, and let his head drop full-face into his soup, like he'd seen too many movies.

    (LAKSHMI does this by cushioning her dropping head with her hands)

Still, if you're a stranger, right?, you tend to be a little slow on the uptake. Without raising his face from that soup, he suddenly pointed behind Smith and went: 'Look!'

    (and)

And when Smith fell for the oldest trick in the book, the flower puff grabbed a handful of papaya, I think, and bolted out the back door, holding his forehead in his free hand and going, 'Ow! Ow! Ow!'

    (LAKSHMI takes off)

Smith didn't even bother chasing. He would never beat the nearest migraine to the fellow anyway. Anyway, bloody Lingayya was right: he wasn't worth it.'

*(Back on play level, LAKSHMI returns and gives SMITH a
huge hug to settle him down.*

Blackout)

15.

*(The looming shape of Kali-Chinnamasta is backlit into
prominence. Throughout it will be highlighted more or less
as necessary.*

Focus comes onto READER SMITH)

READER SMITH: 'That night, Helen, that Nandi Baba night…
Outside, by the fire, the woman Annapurna said, remember?,
Lingayya's men 'kindly' made sure I made it safely to the top of
the mangrove track. I knew where it led, that disgusting sump of a
pool. Full moon. I had no trouble following the track. Plop, plop.
Click-click. Those *sucking* sounds of mangroves… *squelchings*…
that set your teeth on edge.
   (and)
She was sitting there, waiting, maybe halfway down…'

(Lighting up on SMITH coming across ANNAPURNA)

SMITH: So this is it?

ANNAPURNA: No, down at the water's edge.

SMITH: I didn't mean that.

ANNAPURNA: I know what you mean.
   (pointing at his crutch again)
It is high moon. I can see what you mean.

SMITH: Isn't it the whole point?

ANNAPURNA: In a way.

SMITH: (guessing) You wanted to talk to me first.

ANNAPURNA: (again) In a way.

SMITH: Okay, where's the fire? You said it was going to be 'by the fire'.

ANNAPURNA: Down there. By the fire, by the swimming pool.

SMITH: Jesus, you call that a swimming pool?

ANNAPURNA: (shrugging) We all are swimming. It covers us all.

SMITH: It's slush and muck.

ANNAPURNA: (again, simply) It covers us all.

SMITH: You sounds like that old crackpot speaking.

>   *(She shrugs 'so what if it is?')*

SMITH: Is he down there?

>   *(She brightens)*

ANNAPURNA: Where the Baba wishes to complete his forty days and nights with the dead.

SMITH: (cynically) Terrific.

ANNAPURNA: Mr Smith, you should be pleased. It will be the full rites of Tantra.

SMITH: Tantra.

ANNAPURNA: Tantra is All.
    (her voice husky with excitement)
The five All in the one All.

SMITH: All five? That supposed to make the hairs on the back of my neck curl up?

ANNAPURNA: (happily) Yes.

> *(Her pleasure only lasts until her child has a fit of coughing)*

SMITH: That doesn't sound too good.

ANNAPURNA: It will be all right soon.

SMITH: Well, it's good to see you happy.
   (and)
And that's what you're here for, to tell me about these Five Ms?

ANNAPURNA: (nodding) The five ritual of alcohol, fish, grain, meat and, lastly, sexual intercourse. It is very rare, very powerful. You must very careful.

SMITH: The fifth one... are you kidding? *There*? By the edge of that stinking sump?

> *(She only shrugs enigmatically.*
>
> *She draws a grumey coir thread back and forth through her lips. It is an age-old parody of seductiveness that, nonetheless, has the desired unsettling effect on him.*
>
> *She hands it up to him)*

SMITH: What?

ANNAPURNA: It won't hurt you. It has in it the birth cord of a cat that has died after too many kittens. You should keep it for the Tantra time to come. It is blessed with stiffness.

SMITH: No, but who are you?

ANNAPURNA: I was born in Punjab and sent to a convent in Delhi. I was married at sixteen. My husband divorced me because I was giving him three girls, no boys. My father could not afford to keep me with three children and my unmarried sister and aunt. My other two children died on the streets. One day Lord Shiva sent Nandi Baba along to say he would never dream of helping me, so he did.

SMITH: I know all that is bull.

ANNAPURNA: (amused) Isn't it what we women are told to say, aitcha?

SMITH: I've got to ask you... what does that old crackpot know about my son?

ANNAPURNA: Who?

SMITH: Okay, I'll play the game. Nandi Baba. What does he really know?

ANNAPURNA: (shrugging) Your Terry brought him the little ones from the convent.

SMITH: It had to be more than that.

ANNAPURNA: The Baba told me to ignore you if you asked that.

SMITH: Okay, try this: Terry brought the little bodies not to the Baba but thinking it was to the Hag Goddess... the Goddess... right?

ANNAPURNA: Chinnamasta is the bull, the horned cow, and She is the avenger come up. She is the All in the All of the Divine Mother.

SMITH: So?

ANNAPURNA: She returns the bodies back to the parents. She stands on them and eats the baby and makes it go away. Then She washes their sins away.

SMITH: And that's what Nandi Baba thinks he's doing?

ANNAPURNA: Of course.

SMITH: And Nandi Baba 'echoes' this Goddess's okay, how?... He stands on the edge of that filthy bloody pool and swings the little kids around his head by the ankles and then just *flings them in*?

> *(They have to stop while the child has another coughing fit. Anyway, ANNAPURNA is obviously not going to answer him)*

SMITH: She's burning up.

ANNAPURNA: It will be over soon. The Baba will set her free too.

SMITH: You're not going to let him throw her into that pool of gunk? It'll kill her!

ANNAPURNA: No, no. Us.

SMITH: You and me?

ANNAPURNA: (nodding) It has already begun.

SMITH: Like, sure, he sees that.

ANNAPURNA: (pointing at his crutch) He sees *that* as it has begun.

> *(SMITH decides to plunge right in:)*

SMITH: Answer me something: Who's the real father of your child?

ANNAPURNA: It doesn't matter now.

SMITH: You know.

(She only shrugs)

SMITH: It does matter! That young nun, your Smita, saw some disgusting act! Was it that priest, pounce Curlyhead?

(She is stopped up short by his aggression, protects her child by automatic response. The gesture brings him up short)

SMITH: Sorry, sorry.

ANNAPURNA: (barely) It does not matter.

SMITH: (finally) Do you know who Sister Smita was?
    (she turns her face away)
She was my Terry's twin. She was our little Louise.

(She slowly and painfully nods that she knew)

ANNAPURNA: I am so sorry.

SMITH: *They were my children*!

ANNAPURNA: Ssh. Soon, soon.

(SMITH gets himself under better control)

SMITH: So, the father? Father Michael? And you ran and left Smita, or after what happened to Smita, you ran?

ANNAPURNA: It does not matter over All. Over All.

(She looks him straight in the eye)

ANNAPURNA: Nobody knows how your Terry was killed, Mr Smith.

SMITH: Not even your Baba?

ANNAPURNA: (believably) No. Perhaps it was karma.

SMITH: You believe that?

ANNAPURNA: Sometimes. Maybe. Yes.

> (Long pause under the night sounds of the mangroves. Finally, SMITH gives it all up:)

SMITH: You're right. It does and it doesn't matter.

> (He turns and calls to farther down the track)

SMITH: HEY, FATSO! COMING READY OR NOT!

> (Instant on-off blackout, as though a blink of an eye)

16.

> (In that flick of an eyelid, NANDI BABA is now seated next to ANNAPURNA.

> He returns a shout back to SMITH)

NANDI BABA: WHERE'S THE FAGGOT WITH NO BALLS? OO, HEE HEE HEE, HELLO, SAILOR!

> (While SMITH gathers himself, the Baba shoves ANNAPURNA aside. She stays 'out of it' where he has shoved her. SMITH goes to help her up, but she pushes his helping hand away, remains where 'fallen'.

He smooths the ground in front of him and motions SMITH to sit opposite. He is drinking from a bottle of whiskey (maybe) and is chewing away on some cud (or 'golee') while puffing away on a cigar while drawing in the dirt between them.

The lighting emphasises his gross size and how in the full moon and the moving branches his form seems to undulate:)

NANDI BABA: ('sweet as pie')
Om harim kling kandarpa svaha
Om harim krom svaha...
   (then)
Nothing is as frikkered up as nothing! So nothing is a something that ist far wurst than nothing is and you kunst be more ab-soo-bloody-loot-ly more fuchting NOTHING as that! SO WHERE DOES THAT LEAVE YOU, TWERP?!

SMITH: Who are you talking to, Fatso?

NANDI BABA: Hee, hee... der wast a little man and no man who had a little gun und no gun and he saw and did not see ein little bird and no bird on a wire und no wire and he shot und did not shoot der little bird dead and not dead. Missed it by a country shithouse actually. SO WHERE DOES THIS LEAVE YOU STILL, YOU PATHETIC SOMEBODY TWERP?

SMITH: What state did you put my Terry in, bastard?

NANDI BABA: (sweetly) Now you don't mean that, mein herr. But of course you do. You think you are fanny funny? You think you fad while I fart? All ist paradox, good my young master. What you have is a fanny that is not a bubba boy and is not a fanny either 'cause it ist attached to ein little girl nunny gone gurflunkent guttscheissen phfffuttt gerstorben dead down der well, oops. Hey nunny no. Not funny. It is a yoni gone to the Yonder, a little quim gone well quack-quack. What's in a paradox that's not in a paradox? That's the paradox. SO WHERE DOES THIS LAESSEN YOU, TWERP?!

96

SMITH: (screaming at him) Idiot! Idiot!

NANDI BABA: (sweetness again) Say ja for no without making it jarring.

(He holds up a wad of bhang paste)

NANDI BABA: Eat this if you insist on being a SOMEBODY.

SMITH: Bash it.

NANDI BABA: EAT OR I TAKE MY BAT AND BALL UND GO HOME!

(SMITH looks to ANNAPURNA, who pleads with her eyes that he chews it. He does, while:)

SMITH: (painfully) My boy. He was just out of his teens.

NANDI BABA: Piss ovf! Der ist nothing for you here, NOBODY of a FUCHTING SOMEBODY!
   (but)
The chewie... not too spicy, nein?, mein little fahrenden gesellen?

(The moonlight comes on them fully. First NANDI BABA and then SMITH raise their faces to it and 'drift' with it.

The figure of the Hag Goddess grows large temporarily behind and above them)

NANDI BABA: I'm not talking to you anymore, NOBODY, so you'd better listen up, you shitbum full of fartness. All is paradox. True reality is a landscape of no opposites, nothing other than its nothing self. I'm talking to you, you dog bite of a SOMEBODY! Get der wax out, schnell. Fucking remember that in paradox, everything is clever if you are dumb-arsed enough to try, GAWD FRUCK A DRUCK! Or did Gawd, sweetie?
Om harim kling kandarpa svaha
Om harim krom svaha...

(For the moment, Smith finds this logic all right, and that it is all right to nod his perfectly civilised agreement)

SMITH: Ach ja!

NANDI BABA: I'm not talking to you anymore, so you'd better listen up while I do, you dirtbag full of NOTHING. True reality is a landscape of no opposites, nothing other than its nothing self. I'm not talking to you, you damn SOMEBODY. Get der udder sidewax out, schnell. Just remember that in paradox, everything can be deduced...

SMITH: Crap.

NANDI BABA: Smith, you pathetic SOMEBODY, you look sick and you should look sicker. Think of Panadol. Drink. Or not. It does not matter. It does matter. The only real thing is to be splashing around in the eternal Now. That is *summa*, you poor stupid NOBODY. You have to live in summa. You can't live in summa. It is never there. It is always nearly there and nearly not there. You see your dumb problem? You can never reach you und you can never escape you. Big, big paradox, nein?', und again:
Om harim kling kandarpa svaha
Om harim krom svaha...'
    (then)
Boy, you've got a big dicky.

> *(He slaps ANNAPURNA on the shoulder as if she was a naughty girl)*

NANDI BABA: Stop it, vat you are do-ink to this poor man!

(Silence while he sways in the light)

NANDI BABA: Ya, the Final Paradox, und yaboos and yasucks to you, NOBODY!

SMITH: (gathers himself) And the Final Paradox on your Pox on you, stupid old loon!

NANDI BABA: Good, sehr wohl! You work the Final Paradox out yourself, *somebody you nobody. Omkar, omkar.'*

SMITH: You ran from me, fatty.

NANDI BABA: I did not want to run, so I went for a run, you Hanwurst.

SMITH: Kraut.

NANDI BABA: Shrunken pumpernickel!

SMITH: Nutcase square head!

(The BABA half giggles, half screeches with delight)

NANDI BABA: So, mein kleine herr, enough of the pleasantries, sweet prince. What think?

SMITH: You're all teeth.

NANDI BABA: I haf promised you Tantra to your left hand lying through my teeth.'

SMITH: Do your worst, fatso.

NANDI BABA: Drink. We are going to Pooja beyond der graves, past the burnt offerings, ja?, to the place of the unliving and the not-dead. And we will ask a cure for your problems from the Goddess, you stupid NOTHING. Aren't you lucky or would you prefer to be dunked?

SMITH: What you've got, whacko.

NANDI BABA: Eating a human corpse is no more disgusting than anything else.

SMITH: Understood.

NANDI BABA: Eating shit is no more disgusting than eating anything else.

SMITH: Understood.

NANDI BABA: Drinking blood is giving blood und is real dishy.

SMITH: Understood. Your corpse and your shit and your blood and I'll raise you one.

NANDI BABA: You scheizenhausen Himmelsteinhead! You should get a bigger wang or call it weiner. Piss orf! Go down to the flood! Take your time, no hurry. I WILL WAIT HERE!

(But he jumps up with surprising agility and takes off at a sprint.

When he is gone, ANNAPURNA gets up with the child. She stands over SMITH, looks down at him questioningly. She is now openly sexually suggestive, if not downright demanding.

He nods yes he is willing and let her help him to his feet. He can barely walk but gets mobile with her.

They leave in the direction NANDI BABA went.

Blackout.

17.

(Full moon lighting on cess pool.

The Goddess figure is now prominent, featured, 'alive'.

SMITH and NANDI BABA are sitting opposite each other.

ANNAPURNA is sitting with her back to the 'water-sludge'.

In this light, the Baba's body looks huge and white-gross,
slug-like and transgender, as though his breasts were
grossly enlarged and he was showing in the negative)

READER SMITH: (reading 'over') 'Smith smelt the sulphur
miasma of the pool. He saw newly how the Baba was sitting
opposite him now, grunting, pawing the earth. All right. And now
in the one light spun of moonlight, Smith was looking at the
halves of the Baba as man, the halves of the Baba as women, the
halves of him as the Hag Goddess, all in figure on the palm of his
left hand... sprung-light play of them all, the cunnies and cocks,
the trench and the stretch. Or not. Or nodding. It was only, after
all, a nature acceptable as being all right. The Baba scraping his
hooves across the ground in gross itch, growling to be let in.
Om harim kling kandarpa svaha
Om harim krom svaha...
All right. Smith laughed at the moon and thought he laughed. A
swallow of the liquid bhang burnt his tongue, bit into his mind,
called into the moonlight the inner peopled nature of his inner
spaces. All right, all right. He considered he could be smiling.
The Baba was chanting the words that were already in whiz-bang
sonata in bell air:
Om harim krom svaha... '

(As the BABA pours, cuts, draws, performs the Tantra of the
Five Ms, growing loudness and shrillness...)

READER SMITH: (crying out over it all) 'And that was still all
right by Smith... even seeing the blood being poured onto the
warming mud of the swamp he was sitting on -- triangles within
triangles and in the centre of which, Smith knew, was the mystic
eye that sees all, knows all, that does not give a hoot in hell. And
that was all right for Smith too, even as the Baba purified the great
eye with more blood from the moon's chalice, and he came down
the ages, calling the Tantra's five Ms...

NANDI BABA: I cannot speak. I cannot talk. I cannot stop the
true nature of the voice. First, calls you the *madya.*

SMITH: (mad count-down) One! Alcohol! And your six arms are waving!

(He takes a dirty cup with filthy liquid in it from and drinks from it.

The lighting on the place begins to grow darker and darker...

NANDI BABA takes something bloody up from a silver plate, puts it in his mouth lip-smackingly, chews on it, and:)

NANDI BABA: I cannot speak. I cannot talk. I cannot stop the true nature of the voice. Now, calls you the *mamsa*.

SMITH: (ululating) Two! The brain of a puppy! And your six arms are waving!

(NANDI BABA takes the meat from his mouth, squeezes blood out of it onto the ground, passes some of it onto SMITH, who grabs it and eats slavishly.

As he does so, he crazily waves 'come on, come on' to the figure of the Goddess)

READER SMITH: (almost only a voice now) 'Now Smith saw how the Baba's mouth was a black sky, fouled with decay, and its spiked canines tore at the bloody meat chewing the dog flesh into more blood and then throwing it to the end of the triangle of triangles of the yantra, to the end of consciousness itself, their rut song to the Hag rising in heat coming for him then...'

(NANDI BABA tears a chunk off a whole fish with his teeth, chews and spits it out, then works it into the filth of the cesspool)

NANDI BABA: You cannot hear my voice. I cannot talk. I cannot stop the true nature of the voice. Next calls you the *matrya*.

SMITH (ecstatic) Three! The rotting fish! And your six arms are waving!

(He grabs the chewed fish when held out to him and just as ravenously eats this too)

READER SMITH: (rising crescendo) 'And Smith's six or six thousand arms waved in the silent tide of the Hag Chinnamasta, nearly there now at him and coming hot-eyed.'

NANDI BABA: (now shrill) You cannot hear! I cannot talk! I cannot stop the true nature of the voice! Next calls the fourth, the *mudra*!

SMITH: (howling) Four! The sacred hands! And your fucking six arms are fucking waving!

(NANDI BABA slides his hands in and out of the sludge, in and around the objects and the yantra between them, while SMITH rocks, sways backwards, physically opens himself up towards the over-arching Kali-Chinnamasta)

READER SMITH: 'And Smith then let himself slide open to the fourth M, the mudra, the sacred hand gestures, and when they stirred the steaming cesspool where there seemed no Baba at all but instead all was Om Om Om which began the world and would end the world, Kali Chinnamasta...'

NANDI BABA: (in vague enlarging silhouette) I cannot talk, you hear, we come. Now calls you the *maithuna*!...

SMITH: (can't wait) Five! The
     (sexual grunting)
Urh! urh! urh!

(NANDI BABA has disappeared.

SMITH and ANNAPURNA are grabbing wildly in the gloom for each other. They come together with a frenzy...)

READER SMITH: (frantic loud now) 'And Smith lay open for the Hag Goddess to come suckle, come rut. He swayed before Her sad bones and Her sad skulls Her sad milkless swinging tits, Her bat-wing cunny lips moisture-none. She screeched for him. She slobbered for him. She smeared dung over him, dog shit to his chest...'

(SMITH and ANNAPURNA are now in frot, thrashing around in the mud by the side of the cess pool.

A silhouetted shape looms out of the darkness towards them. It is not just the Hag Goddess's form, but something growing huge, with an enormous horned head. It hovers about them, fog-bound, over-powering, killingly...)

READER SMITH: 'The fifth M, the *maithuna*, the intercourse! And Smith wide-open with the woman Annapurna, as steeled as a rod, as granite-got as the shrine, feeling the Hag Goddess trembling rabidly above into them, slurping, clawing Her own neck, maddened with being eternally excluded! But that was all right! He was hot to be cold blood. Teasingly he pushed the life he had; he withdrew it! He pushed life, withdrew it.! He listened nicely to the Hag's frantic shrieks!...

(Now the bull-human form bellows climactically. It swoops down with brutish intent and sweeps up ANNAPURNA's child as rightful sacrifice/penance. It looks for all the world as it is about to tear the girl's throat out with its bare teeth.

But, in a sudden bettering light, ANNAPURNA wrenches herself away from SMITH, beating at him to let her go, then launches herself murderously at NANDI BABA to rescue her child. The child is let go, falls on SMITH.

Still, ANNAPURNA and NANDI BABA grapple each other with abject fury. She has torn off his bull headgear to reveal it is the old priest.

They reel into the cess pool, refusing to let go of one another. Their momentum has taken them beyond easy depth. Locked together they cannot gain footing. But on the 'shore' SMITH is too disorientated to be able to help; it is all he can do to stop the child from rolling down the mud-slippery bank into the water herself.

The BABA and ANNAPURNA have not made any sound, but have torn at each other in a vast mortal embrace. They sink, thrashing, in the same way.

There is sudden silence.

Blackout)

18.

READER SMITH: (finally, very quietly) Helen, it was as if that ooze only wanted to stir slightly in irritation before returning to the deadened. And Smith understood that was all right too. After all, it was the Pooja -- the new moon when even cesspools shine brightly. And who held tightly to him, he could see, was who their damnable wheel turn-turning had it to be.

(Blackout)

19.

(It is very early morning. The lighting comes up in SMITH's room back at the boarding house, where the very muddy child is sleeping in his bed.

SMITH opens the door for LAKSHMI and SINGH, who are in their night attire.

They take one look at the child and both dash to her.

SINGH ensures her health while LAKSHMI, needing only to take a brief look, hurries off obviously to an en-suite bathroom for towels and soap and water.

SMITH, dishevelled and filthy, stands back sheepishly and not a little unsteadily due to a hang-over.)

SMITH: (as though his fault) She has diarrhoea, sorry.

(The Singhs take no notice of him)

SMITH: She has real bad fever, sorry.

(They take no notice of him)

SMITH: I wanted to clean her up but I didn't want to... you know. Sorry.

(If they take any notice of him, it is only to look right through him.

SINGH straightens, hurries out, brushing unapologetically past SMITH. He is going for his doctor's 'bag'.

In the interim:)

READER SMITH: 'Nandi Baba. They must have put so much pressure on him that he got the goofy idea of being the Goddess's go-between to free everybody from sin. Who could possibly carry that burden? Don't tell me he didn't go mad and start believing he really was the Goddess with the power of redemption and resurrection in his fat hands. He should have stuck with Tantra trickles. I mean, taking on the sins of the world on his fat old shoulders like that... if that filthy place was the Sea of Gallilee, they would've filled his net with fish... and then thrown *him* back. Should I be joking about him? Helen, frankly, I don't know. But forgive, forgive anyway.'

(He fades.

SMITH edges fearfully towards the girl. She weakly holds out a hand to him. With a choked cry of relief he crosses to her to hold her hand, kneeling down to her level)

SMITH: (tremolo) Louise?

(After a while, the child nods)

SMITH: Louise.

(The child nods again)

SMITH: (joyfully up at LAKSHMI) From the moment I called her that, she opened her eyes.
     (back to the girl)
Louise. Yes. It's all right.

(He holds onto her hand with both of his.

LAKSHMI returns not long before SINGH does. They go about administering to the child and the bed. SMITH is shouldered out of the way very promptly. She does not hesitate in busying herself as she goes about her business of washing the girl down)

LAKSHMI: She is very erky in the wrong places, Mr Smith.

SMITH: Sorry.

LAKSHMI: It is okeydokey, Mr Smith.

SMITH: I can't remember getting her back.

LAKSHMI: The Singhs have always encouraged sleeping strongly down through the ages. Isn't that right, Dr Singh?

(This is to SINGH who returns, as professional and busy as she is)

SINGH: (automatically) Absolutely, my dear.

*(He does another quick assessment of the child, then gives
her a shot of antibiotics)*

SMITH: (almost outcry) I should remember bringing her back.

LAKSHMI: It is good you didn't, Mr Smith.

SINGH: Hello?, that's true.

*(The doctor has brought not only has his medical bag but
clean sheets. Together, they replace the bedding expertly.*

*Before, though, LAKSHMI gently 'disconnects' SMITH and
the girl's hands. When they have finished with changing the
sheets, she comes back and 'connects' them just as gently.*

*SMITH has to release the child's hand anyway, stands back,
his face in his hands)*

LAKSHMI: You will want to tell us what happened, Mr Smith.
You should not tell us what happened.

SINGH: Hello?, no.

LAKSHMI: We can leave all that to the Inspector, which makes
the best sense.

SINGH: (at least directly to him) He had some of his men there in
the mangroves just in case. To watch out for you, I would have
thought. They took you there in the first place, no?

SMITH: Where were they? Where *are* they?

LAKSHMI: Oh, they would have been around, Mr Smith.

SINGH: Hello, hello? It was the tantra, Mr Smith. It is best to
stay away from the tantra, don't you know.

LAKSHMI: And I dare say your mouth is all full of mud, is it not, Mr Smith?

SMITH: (sotto voce) I called her Louise, and she nodded.

LAKSHMI: Yes, you said. Sometimes even the tinies know where that thar wind blows, isn't that so, Dr Singh.

SINGH: Absolutely, my dear.

(They stand back, finished)

LAKSHMI: There. Dr Singh, you may put some clothes on, I think. Mr Smith won't mind me staying here in my night dress which doesn't see through to anything Australians have not seen before on their naked cows. Mr Smith, you go and pull up a chair and you hold that child's hand until the Inspector comes a-thundering in over the rise like the hoo-ha cavalry, pardner.

(SINGH inspects the girl one more time, nods, and goes to leave. He is stopped by his wife:)

LAKSHMI: Oh, and Dr Singh, I think it might he high time for a certain report...?

SINGH: You mean, I think, the autopsy?

LAKSHMI: (long suffering) Yes, Dr Singh.

SINGH: Hello?, coming right up, my dear.

(SMITH and LAKSHMI sit in silence watching over the girl. Finally:)

LAKSHMI: Mr Smith, you should go and ablute and lather up so that the girl can have better memories of you when she wakes. Australians always feel better when they wash their mouths out with soap, a specialty of this establishment.

(He doesn't want to leave her for a moment)
109

LAKSHMI: She will be hunky-dory, Mr Smith.

(When LINGAYYA, in full uniform, unceremoniously crashes open the door. Yet he only sternly looks in, takes in the scene, and brusquely points his lathi and the girl in the bed)

LAKSHMI: (to answer him) She's quite all right, Inspector.

(He swings his lathi towards SMITH)

LAKSHMI: He is all right too. It's just how Australians look in the mornings, don't you know.

(LINGAYYA nods, having to be satisfied with those answers, then leaves, slamming the door behind him.

(Blackout.)

20.

(A day later. Lighting up on boarding house room.

The girl is still huddled in bed, holding SMITH's hand as if she will never let go. She is now all cleaned up, wrapped in spotless bed linen.

LAKSHMI and SINGH sit patiently waiting.

In this 'frieze', emerges READER SMITH. He is half-whispering, reflective of the mood:)

READER SMITH: 'But Smith came to remember and, for one of the few times in his life, Helen, exactly. While the crabs plopped and there shone shafts brighter than the sun and sadder-sad, he had lifted the child out of there. Such a feather weight for her age. Such a nothing weight he knew he could carry at last. And he carried her away across his chest, as her mother always had. At least he knew where his feet were leading him in the soon-silvering early night of that shaping and nodding and wisest of full moons. He only felt Lingayya's men brush past him but they were soon gone away from him too. In his urgency to get where there wasn't any rush -- and that was just another paradox. And if so, thereby Nandi-Baba-blessed, he had to be heading in the right direction. He knew at last what he wanted was to actually be, then. But, still, he wasn't quite where he wanted to be yet...'

   (Focus back on the play area)

SMITH: (undemanding) Did you say you'd finished the report? Or just finishing?

SINGH: Hello?, finished. The Inspector is just logging it in and will bring it over, Mr Smith.

SMITH: Can I be sure I can send Terry home?

LAKSHMI: You betcha bottom's dollar! Melbourne's just a hop, skip and a jump away for properly-sent coffin from our region here. We've got it down pat, kiddo.

SMITH: No, to Sri Lanka. To his mother.

LAKSHMI: Ah, she is a lucky woman, Mr Smith.

SMITH: No she isn't.

LAKSHMI: She is not so much a lucky woman, Mr Smith, but lucky all the same.

SINGH: Hello, hello?, my dear...

LAKSHMI: We have a money-back guarantee about dispatch and arrival of coffins when it comes to not being ashes, Mr Smith.

SINGH: (admonish) Hello, hello?, my dear.

SMITH: (flatly) Yeah, you having a funeral parlour business as well is a great help.

SINGH: The guests almost demanded it, so what to do?.

LAKSHMI: (to SMITH) So you see, you mustn't be so down-crested, you dear man.

SINGH: (proudly) And soon the business premises will be relocated to the other side of our front door to the clinic.

SMITH: Births on one side. Death on the other.

SINGH: Precisely!

SMITH: I can think of the signs.

SINGH: Absolutely!

LAKSHMI: Our finest will be used in their composition, you have the tip of this nose on that, Mr Smith.

SMITH: They will be magnificent signs.

>   *(The child coughs. They each stiffen, wait. But it doesn't develop into anything bad)*

SMITH: Can I ask something?
   (to their waiting)
It's real common what happens to a lot of infant girls here, which isn't my business. But I was just wondering... you two so kind and big-hearted and all that... how come running one of the so-called fertility clinics.

LAKSHMI: I think Mr Smith is referring to that beep-beep contraption of yours, Dr Singh.

SINGH: (defensive) Hello?, what's 'contraption' about it?

LAKSHMI: That it goes beep-beep I would say instead of hello good day. Isn't that what you mean, Mr Smith?

SMITH: One beep for a he, two for a little she, sort of thing?

LAKSHMI: (with SMITH) That sort of contraption, Dr Singh.

SINGH: (grumpy) It's beep-beep for all, don't you know.

(They could even be close to a slight disagreement)

SMITH: I was sort of meaning how the beep-beeps sort of lead to... you know...

LAKSHMI: Some ladies leaving with less in the belly than they came in with. Is that what we mean, Mr Smith?

SMITH: (nodding) I mean, do some of them really ask for brown-paper-bag take-aways?

LAKSHMI: I call them abortions to their faces, Mr Smith. I say to them you hussies you; you just thank your lucky stars you're paying customers.

SINGH: Hello, hello!

LAKSHMI: I am comforted in myself that our brown paper bags have our logo on them. At least there we run a tidy ship, Mr Smith.

SINGH: Hello, hello?, someone has to make it safe and cheap enough for the unfortunates, remember, Mrs Singh?
    (to SMITH)
Terry understood.

SMITH: (sharply) No, he wouldn't have!

(A really awkward pause)

LAKSHMI: (beaming at SMITH) Sometimes one forgets the
good that one does, Mr Smith!
   (then gushes)
And right now we are using our own money to have our daughter-
in-law treated in Mumbai. You heard it first here, Mr Smith!

>*(This lets the cat out of the bag. SMITH is quite staggered
>by the news of sending their own away and to have what
>sounds like a predetermined termination)*

SINGH: (desperate to be understood) Hello?, Mr Smith, Smithee...
it's not just that it's bad luck to have a girl first. What if there is
only a girl?

>*(LAKSHMI gasps, clamps the palms of her hands together,
>raises them to her forehead, and bows before Smith in total
>abjection in the traditional meekest of Hindu ways)*

READER SMITH: 'That kindly woman, who had the day before
finished cleaning up my Louise and preparing her as best she
could for the journey, was begging Smith, crude and uncivilised a
human being by any comparison, to try to understand the complexi-
ties of her country. As if Smith was possibly polished enough for
that'

SINGH: Smithee... if by the will of Lord Shiva, my son is sonless,
then we could well have all our property, everything, pass on to
our own granddaughter's inlaws one day. How do we know who
they are? There is a saying here. Hello?, it is: "Raising a daughter
is tending someone else's garden".
   (and)
When we get old, who will look after us, if we have no sons or
grandsons and our only daughter is living somewhere else looking
after some strangers?

SMITH: (appalled he asked) Doctor, Madam... I didn't mean to...

SINGH: No, Mr Smith, maybe you don't understand. When I
die... *who will light my pyre*?!

(LAKSHMI bursts into tears. Here is great sorrow bursting out.

SMITH untangles himself from his Louise as fast as he can, hurries to LAKSHMI and clasped her clasped hands. With SINGH's permission, he kisses her forehead)

SMITH: Dear lady, may your daughter-in-law be the mother of a hundred sons.

(LAKSMHI's eyes go as large as promised moons at the sudden, wonderful prospect)

LAKSHMI: Get on with you flirtatious Aussies.

(The girl rolls over, cuddles more into SMITH's side, who has hurried back to her. It relieves the pressure of the conversation.

Further wait for LINGAYYA, until it is left to SINGH to know how to break the ice:)

SINGH: Give us a little dance, my dear?

LAKSHMI: (false coy) Oh, you men.

SINGH: To relieve our weary bones, Mrs Singh. To make the child and us all get better more quickly here and in Mumbai.

LAKSHMI: But only if everyone present realises they have seen it first in this bedroom at the top of these stairs.

SINGH: Hello?, absolutely, my dear.

(LAKSHMI takes off her sandals and dances for them.

She starts out with a heavy heart and heavily, but then soon seems to become lighter, back to her flighty self.

SINGH claps her basic timing.

*As heavy as her thighs were at the beginning she is soon
spinning and twisting and ooh'ing and aah'ing the love-sick
unrequites of the Lord Shiva to his maidens. She echoes the
rhythm clicking her own tongue; her arms waving and her
hand movements in intricate mudras)*

LAKSHMI:
*On all my limbs
Were spells of love.
What strength I needed
To arrest desire...*

> *(She finishes only when she cannot control her panting due
> to her size, but even this seems a message of desire.*
>
> *SINGH grabs her hand as though he would never get
> another chance to bend low and kiss it. She doesn't giggle
> or roll her eyes; rather she stands there looking down at
> him exquisitely)*

SMITH: (softly) Thank you.

> (Momentary frieze, for:)

READING SMITH: 'And even while the Singhs closed in and
around each other, Smith felt the surety that beyond the guest
house somewhere, out on the perimeter of their wheel's rim, there
was a speeding up and there was still time to climb aboard it to go
finally where he wanted to go and to find out the most important
thing in his life.'

> *(LINGAYYA comes into the room without waiting to be
> invited. He is in full uniform.*
>
> *He sniggers at the Singhs holding on to each other, then at
> SMITH holding onto the child)*

LINGAYYA: (to SMITH) I see for once you got somewhere on
time, *puta*.

116

SMITH: How would you know?

LINGAYYA: Only by you being too late to stop your son from *picking* and evidently too late to save the Nandi Baba and...
     (points to child)
the mother.

SMITH: *Hey!* This little girl's awake.

LINGAYYA: Good, she can help me clean up your mess.

(SMITH is brought up short on the possible meaning that LINGAYYA might be going to detain him, or worse)

SMITH: Are you saying you can help?

LINGAYYA: Relax, *picker*.

LAKSHMI: We are all friendly guests of the boarding house, aren't we not, guys?

LINGAYYA: Okay, okay. I said relax.

(He brandishes the autopsy report, rounds on SINGH)

LINGAYYA: You should light a fire under that typist of yours.

LAKSHMI: (excited) Did you notice it too?

LINGAYYA: I noticed it.

SINGH: What?

LAKSHMI: My precious, before you touch any more signs you have to employ a proofreader all over the shop.

SINGH: (still clueless) Hello?, what?

(LINGAYYA thrusts the report into SMITH's hands)

LINGAYYA: You tell him.

(SMITH takes it, can't catch onto anything he should, it seems)

SMITH: ('cannot') It's in Hindi or Malayalam or something.

LAKSHMI: (as though to a child) Mr Smith, the English bits, you old silly. With apologies for the...
    (stresses)
typing mistakes be my poor dear ball-and-chain needs better glasses for.
    ('Hollywood' mock shock)
Oo, stiff cheese, honey pie.

SINGH: (getting annoyed) Hello, what?

LAKSHMI: Hurry, Mr Smith. There is much to be done before tonight's plane.
    (inquiry to LINGAYYA)
It still is tonight's plane, isn't it, Inspector?

LINGAYYA: ('get rid of him') The sooner the pissing...
    (stops when she clicks her tongue)
sorry... better.

LAKSHMI: Mind you, I think we all deserve a little swear word or two, don't you, Dr Singh dear?

SINGH: (still out of the loop) Hello, hello?, I say again: what?

(SMITH gets an inkling of what she and LINGAYYA are talking about:)

SMITH: Okay, I get 'Mrs Terry J. Smith' instead of 'Mr Terry J. Smith'...?

LAKSHMI: (clap hands) You clevery, you!

SINGH: (still clueless) Old manual typewriters. What to do there? Half the bulbs not working and she must be the only typist who refuses to learn to type. Hello?

LAKSHMI: (can't contain herself) Think, Mr Smith, or I'll bust my bra!

SINGH: (rebuke) Hello?, excuse me.

LAKSHMI: Don't be silly, my dear. Have you ever seen me bust my bra?

SINGH: Not yet, no.

LINGAYYA: (re SMITH) Show the dope. I haven't got all day.

LAKSHMI: Are you still over hung, Mr Smith?

SMITH: Probably.

(She goes over to tap autopsy report)

LAKSHMI: 'Mrs' means 'Mrs'.

SMITH: (still not getting it) Okay.

LAKSHMI: (now back at home) So it seems you have been travelling with your wife, you naughty not-telling man... now, in the nicking of time, my clever husband has produced his autopsy report that has allowed our sharp-eyed-like-a-hawk Inspector... who is a real doll really and really brawny when you get to know him in his banyan if he was the last man in the world... to add an official Police travel pass just for you and this little one.

> *(She flashes great histrionics to introduce LINGAYYA's police letter-of-authority, which he pulls out of his uniform and thrusts into her hands.*
>
> *She takes it and poses to read it:)*

119

LAKSHMI: Mr Smith, I am about to read that letter. Are we all sitting comfortably? It is in translation on the run, so pardon piggy.
    (reads)
'To Who it...' that should read 'Whom' of course but few Customs people, even in India, will reject it on that, aitcha?... 'blah blah... the child, subject of this letter, is the victim of the recent death by persons unknown of her mother and passport holder,
    (emphasizes)
Mrs Terry Smith, while on holiday. See autopsy report attached, darted...
    (clicks tongue re another typing error)
dated 28 May...' That is not right, either, Inspector.

SINGH: Hello, hello?, it's the same typist, my dear.

LINGAYYA: (growl) Who cares?

LAKSHMI: 'The child is travelling with her father'... blah, blah... 'Due to her traumatic experience, the child should be given all due consideration to return home urgently to in Melbourne, Austria'
    (rounds on LINGAYYA)
Australia, Lordie Lordie, Inspector... you too?

LINGAYYA: Just get on with it.

LAKSHMI: '... Signed by Inspector of Police (Kollam) M. N. Lingayya under seal'.

    (SMITH realises the implication)

SMITH: (quite stunned) I can take her out of the country without papers?

LAKSHMI: Yes!

SMITH: And get her through Australian Immigration.

    (LAKSHMI looks momentarily quizzically at LINGAYYA. He answers as much as his latent gruffness will allow)
120

LINGAYYA: ('yes') We will contact them ahead with the details.

(SMITH leaves the child, goes over to LINGAYYA and extends his hand. LINGAYYA allows himself to shake hands, goes over to the girl and pats her head.

He nods to the Singhs and then leaves unceremoniously with his usual gruffness.

SMITH goes over to hug SINGH first)

SINGH: Hello, Smithee? I think you should be hugging my shortsighted typist.

(SMITH next goes to LAKSHMI. He stands before her for a moment, before dropping down and touching her feet in Indian style. This is not quite proper and she quickly pulls him to his feet and gives him an enveloping hug)

SMITH: Madam, may your flower beds always be tended by your loving own.

(This makes her very happy and a lovely presence. She too takes a quick look at the child to see that nothing can at that moment be done.

She turns, hugs SINGH's arm and:)

LAKSHMI: Come, Dr Singh. I think Mr Smith and his daughter should spend some free guest time which won't go on the bill.
    (quickly)
Is 'free' right there, Mr Smith?

SMITH: It is, Mrs Singh.

LAKSHMI: Call me Lakshmi.

SMITH: I have.

LAKSHMI: Have you?

SMITH: I have in my heart.

(The Singhs leave in joint delight.

SMITH has a lot of fussing around and packing to do, while...)

READING SMITH: 'And there it was Helen. Only once between Chennai and Melbourne did her dysentery threaten to give her real sickness away. It helped that Lakshmi Singh had sprayed perfume all over her at the departure gate as though the best strategy was smoke screen. Her lovely little eyes were as large as full moons.
　　(and)
There is not even any Immigration breach to be uncovered unless they dig down to birth dates. Immigration have always had us down as the Smiths returning from India long ago with an adopted boy and an adopted girl even though we didn't. My Louise. My little she. And I have to tell you: long ago came 'Father' in English and long ago came 'Dad'. One day, when she really wants to say 'Mother', I'll try to explain her mother to her. This time round I won't take the coward's way out.
　　(then)
Helen, I know I didn't find out about what happened to our Terry. I grieve about that. And I didn't find out if our lost Louise/Smita was pushed or fell down that damn well, and I grieve about that too. But I feel I have come back right and I know I now will never stop feeling I am right where I've always wanted to be. Sorry, sorry. There I go, apologizing again.

(lighting fades)

(End)